MW01196625

All photos were taken by Tiffany Harelik with the exception of the following:
p 9, 178 Melanie Wright Photography
p 27 Carol Highsmith
p 30, 71, 81 Troy Myatt
p 87 Melanie Kratovil
p 95 Maurine Winkley
p 90, 110, 161 Jennifer Boomer Photography
p 112 WW Foster
p 169 Steve Tremayne
p 173 Mirt Foster

**SPELLBOUND
PUBLISHERS**

THE TERLINGUA CHILI COOKBOOK
CHILI'S LAST FRONTIER

by Tiffany Harelik

PRAISE FOR

The Terlingua Chili Cookbook:
Chili's Last Frontier

"Tiffany Harelik has distinguished herself in the Austin food community with her tireless and influential support of the mobile food trailer trend. Her latest work further proves what I have known for some time: she is a great writer and an unrequited foodie. That's what make this book such a fun and compelling read. She is drawing on first hand experience, not the anecdotal approach one so often sees. I highly recommend her latest work and look forward to having a go at some of the recipes."

-Rob Balon, KLBJ Restaurant Critic, Dining Out with Rob Balon.com

"Starting in Terlingua and spreading across the southwest, we Texans pretended chili was important for so long that it eventually came true - it is. Tiffany Harelik perfectly captures the histories, the yarns, the recipes, and the fun. Whether or not you ever plan to cook a pot of chili, you'd be a damn fool not to read this gem!"

-Harold Cook, progressive political analyst, Capital Tonight Show,
Letters from Texas

ALSO BY TIFFANY HARELIK

COOKBOOKS
The Big Bend Cookbook
The Columbus Food Truck Cookbook with Renee Casteel Cook
Trailer Food Diaries Cookbook: Austin volume 1
Trailer Food Diaries Cookbook: Austin volume 2
Trailer Food Diaries Cookbook: Austin volume 3
Trailer Food Diaries Cookbook: Portland volume 1
Trailer Food Diaries Cookbook: Portland volume 2
Trailer Food Diaries Cookbook: Dallas / Fort Worth edition
Trailer Food Diaries Cookbook: Houston edition
www.tiffanyharelik.com

COVER DESIGN & PHOTOGRAPHY BY
Tom Kirsch Design

This book is dedicated to the resilient people of the Terlingua ghost town, the colorful folks on the chili trail who make the annual trek to Terlingua, and all those who love the Big Bend area. Special distinction is reserved for Glen Felts.

TABLE OF CONTENTS

Chili Recipes, continued

Chili Accompaniment Recipes..162

WELCOME

BIENVENIDOS

TO **TERLINGUA**

GHOSTOWN

TEXAS

BIRTH PLACE TO ALL CHILI COOK OFFS WORLD WIDE

Please
- RESPECT PRIVATE RESIDENCES _____
- USE LITTER CONTAINERS _____
- NO OVERNIGHT PARKING _____
- NO METAL DETECTORS _____
- LEAVE ROCKS, PLANTS, ARTIFACTS _____

Enjoy your Visit

National Register of Historic Places

ACKNOWLEDGEMENTS

Thank you to Harold for taking me to the Texas Chili Parlor for a bowl of venison chili and also for introducing me to Gordon Fowler over a bowl of queso. Thanks to Gordon and Kathleen: two second generation Terlingua chili aficionados whose stories about their dads gave this project real pulse and to all those who contributed their time in sharing their memories.

Special thanks also to Deanna for taking me under her wing in Terlingua; your recipe remains my favorite in this book. Thanks also to Roger for sharing his materials, time, and wisdom so that this project is historically accurate and also for connecting me with some great folks on the chili trail. Thank you to the Liddell family for hosting me on so many of my research trips out west and sharing so many sunsets and dinners together.

Thanks also to the team at Spellbound Publishers whose professional expertise and teamwork made this book more than just stories and recipes but added historical and cre- ative elements that made this title everything I had hoped it would be. Marcy, Tom, Letitia, I am proud of what we did together.

Finally, to my friends and family and all those who have tested recipes with me and helped me navigate the rough patches in cooking and in life: thank you, I love you. It takes just one person supporting your ideas to make them blossom; I am fortunate to have so many.

MY STORY

My first foray into the cookbook world was a project to preserve a few old family recipes. A friend gave me one of her family cookbooks, and it was an old-fashioned inspiration. I knew I wanted to do something similar to preserve my family's kitchen traditions and lore.

The project ballooned into a massive collection of stories and ingredients that I warehoused on my laptop for several years. Eventually, I edited the recipes and in the end, created a keepsake family cookbook to share with future generations. It was then that I realized I had a formula for writing cookbooks and enjoyed doing it.

A dozen cookbooks later, I had written *The Big Bend Cookbook* which came out in October 2014. After I had eaten at the Starlight, stayed in Lajitas, and explored the ghost town cemeteries, I felt like the Terlingua story in *The Big Bend Cookbook* remained somewhat untold. It dawned on me that there were enough stories from the Terlingua region to warrant a separate book altogether. So, I began researching the iconic Terlingua chili cook-off.

My friend Harold Cook (a chili enthusiast with a firm no beans policy) introduced me to the Terlingua cook-off founder's son, painter Gordon Fowler, over a bowl of queso in South Austin. Gordon was in between paintings and was able to surface for a happy hour meeting. Over a drinks, he shared a few stories from the early Terlingua chili days.

As he tells it, when Gordon was in Vietnam someone came to him with a newspaper article covering the inaugural Terlingua chili cook-off. One of the soldiers thought that he recognized Gordon's father in the article and asked Gordon about it. "And, it was!" he tells me stirring the chorizo a little deeper into the communal queso. Gordon obliged my request for a more thorough interview and said I could come over to dig through some old pictures once I got ready to write the book. He recommended reading *A Bowl of Red* by Frank X. Tolbert and *The Great Chili Confrontation* by H. Allen Smith—must-reads for anyone interested in the topic and both of which my dad had stuffed in my Christmas stocking that year.

In addition to those books, I read *Around Terlingua* by Thomas C. Alex and Robert E. Wirt, and *Texas is Chili Country* by Judy Alter. Roger Foltz sent me a copy of Sam Pendergast's *Chili Requiem* and Tom Nall sent me a copy of his book *"Texas Cowboy Cookin': Tom Nall & Texas at the Smithsonian"*. With these on my shelf, I continued to read about chili throughout the writing of this book.

The way I see it, the lore behind the Terlingua chili cook-off is as important as the recipes themselves. The local community survives and thrives year round, but a very different vibe takes over during the cook-off weekend. It is my hope that the reader enjoys not only a slice of Terlingua life but also gets an appreciation for the recipes and histories of the cook-off in the far West Texas desert.

There's an old saying: They aren't making any new old friends. Well, they aren't making any new old chili competitions either. The Terlingua chili cook-off embodies an event pulsing with a lifeblood as thick and rich as the chili the competitors turn out year after year. The competition celebrates its fiftieth anniversary in 2016 and although it has split into three separate factions, traditions of the chili culture will live on through the next generation of cooks. With all the interesting people and stories involved on the chili trail, I could have continued writing this book another year. It is my hope wthat this book preserves the history, people and recipes of the greatest chili cook-off in Texas for all to enjoy.

TERLINGUA, TEXAS – POPULATION 58

The former mining-town-turned-ghost-town is home to an international brawl in the desert where the best chili-makers have brought their recipes for a shot at bragging rights every first Saturday of November since 1967. Over ten thousand "chili-heads" from around the world descend upon the small town to partake in the annual contest, but outside of the cook-off weekend, Terlingua proper is a small community that is home to less than one hundred. It is hot, desolate, and prickly. One false step could land you in a cactus patch, and one wrong turn could lead you into the forgotten quick-silver mines of the past. It takes a particular kind to live there year round, but those who do wouldn't trade it for any other spot on the globe.

Those who call Terlingua home are a patchwork of seekers, hippies, cowboys, homesteaders, off-the-gridders, hotel owners, shopkeepers, artists, dog lovers, and adventurers and probably some folks hoping to live in obscurity. When the sun comes up, you'll see the Mule Ears Peaks and the Chisos Mountains in Big Bend as well as the Santa Fe de Los Pinos mountain range in Mexico over your coffee cup. When the sun sets, someone will start strumming a tune on an old guitar on the porch by the Starlight Theatre. Beer cans start to pop open as the stars flood the night sky. What locals do to pass the hours between sunrise and sunset varies from manning the gas station to working at the grocery store.

Others paint or play music, waitress, hike, work, raft, kayak, drink, host visitors, and everything in between.

My friend Harold once told me, "Look, Marfa is where you go to get discovered; Terlingua is where you go to get lost."

The name Terlingua comes from the Spanish phrase "Tres Lingues" (meaning three languages) referring to the three languages spoken by the area Indian tribes: Kiowa, Apache, and Comanche. The Terlingua automobile racing team also honors the Indian tribes incorporating three feathers into their black and yellow logo that also features a rabbit. As the story goes, the rabbit with its paw extended into the air, is signaling a halt to the addition of more peppers into its chili.

Created by Bill Neale, the logo first appeared on a Ford Mustang developed by Carroll Shelby and driven by Ken Miles in 1965 at Green Valley Raceway in Dallas. The logo became the official symbol of the Terlingua Racing Team for Carroll Shelby's renowned racing adventures, including its appearance on Jerry Titus's Mustang, which won the 1967 Trans Am series the same year as the first Terlingua chili cook-off.

Diego Palacios, co-owner and chef behind the iconic Starlight Theatre, moved to the basin in February of 2001. "There's a population of about 250 in the area," he says, "but once fall comes along, a lot of river guides and waitstaff come back. During that period, there are another 200 people that come down seasonally. You gotta spend at least a couple summers here to be considered a local," Diego says with a winsome smile.

The town of Terlingua has two schools—Terlingua Elementary (grades Pre-K–8) and Big Bend High School (grades 9–12). On average, less than one hundred students are enrolled in first through twelfth grades. Every student that graduates from high school who wants to go to college receives a substantial scholarship from the Chili Appreciation Society International (CASI). On average ten students graduate each year.

Starlight co-owner and second generation Terlinguan Bill Ivey shares that Terlingua was the largest town in the area

during its heyday. "During the mining years, the population was over two thousand," he says, "which would have
surpassed Alpine at that time. Terlingua was the largest
community in the area. It was a bustling community with
two schools. We even had the first ice cream parlor in West
Texas." He says the town was very segregated between the
Mexican laborers and the white workers who typically held
higher ranking positions.

Terlingua became more densely populated during the '70s.
"Because of the national park, there were a lot of people
coming through wanting access to the river. River companies and guides started popping up and charting it out. The
water, then, was much higher than it is today."

Bill shares that his dad Rex Ivey Junior was a Terlingua pioneer and relocated there from Lometa, a Central Texas town,
when he was in his twenties. Rex came to the Big Bend as
a trapper and a fur buyer working all along the Rio Grande.
He bought the town of Lajitas in 1949, bringing the first
gas pump and telephone to the border town. He farmed,
ranched, owned a candelilla wax factory, and served as the
Brewster County Commissioner for more than twenty years.
After selling Lajitas in 1977, Rex and Bill bought the Terlingua
ghost town with the purpose of restoring it.

"He [Rex] was one of the very few people that would ven-
ture into wild territory," Bill explains. "I mentioned my dad
was a pioneer, but even in the '70s, we were still pioneering
the area. I refer to it often as the last frontier."

"You can be who you want to be down here," says Bill with
his big grin.

Diego says that one thing that makes Terlingua unique is that
everyone is welcome as long as they don't do harm to other
people. "It's such a tight community," he says. "Everyone
leaves the car keys in their ignition and never locks the front
door. Everyone watches over and respects each other."

The Starlight Theatre is perhaps the most iconic spot to dine,
drink, and dance to live music for locals and tourists alike.
Their brunch menu features a Monte Christo sandwich, hue-

vos rancheros, chorizo burgers, chicken-fried steak and eggs, quiche, and sweet potato pecan waffles. The lunch menu features a variety of light salads as well as hearty sandwiches and burgers. For dinner, guests enjoy the chicken-fried antelope strips with Lone Star beer gravy, wild boar and venison sausage stuffed with jalapeños and cheese, and other fine fare such as Alaskan salmon and filets mignons. And what first-timer could resist ordering a cup of award-winning Terlingua chili with cheese and onions?

"This building was built in the 1930s as an actual theater: The Chisos Movie Theatre," Bill explains. "As a kid, I remember seeing the holes [in the wall] for the movies to shine through. The Starlight didn't have a roof: that's where the name came from. When it rained, there would be a pond in the middle, and the kids would go swimming. When it was cold, we would have fires in burn barrels." Bill got hassled for putting a roof on the structure in 1993, but he says the building would have fallen had it not been shored up. "I got damned a lot for doing it," he says, "but once it was done, folks appreciated a place to come [into] out of the rain.

"You'll notice when I did the restoration, I left the walls the way they were." People ask him often about the weathered adobe walls. "It's the erosion from the water coming down. It's one of a kind. You can't replicate this kind of stuff."

Bill got involved with the Starlight to preserve the buildings and the culture of the area and the ghost town. "It was beginning to be cut up in half-acre and one-acre tracts, and I felt that would destroy it," Bill says. "I could see a lot of potential, and I love to restore old buildings and furniture, so it gave me a job. In fact, it was a little more than I bargained for, but I'm doing what I love."

Dwight Yoakum probably gives the best description of the feelings Terlingua conjures up in his song "A Thousand Miles from Nowhere":

> I'm a thousand miles from nowhere, time don't matter to me. 'Cause I'm a thousand miles from nowhere, and there's no place I want to be.

"Looking straight ahead you'll never see it," Gary P. Nunn

describes the town in his recording of "Terlingua Sky" and Jerry Jeff Walker pays tribute to the town in his album *Viva Terlingua*. One visit to the old town will explain why artists are inspired to write about the mystique of Terlingua.

Terlingua draws many artists and musicians to the area. Bill explains, "There's infinite inspiration here at all levels. We have incredible musicians that play here at the Starlight. A lot of singer-songwriters are drawn to the area. They are free spirits. Maybe when they play here, they feel like they used to feel in Austin in the old days."

Although anyone can pick up a guitar on the porch, people ask to play at the Starlight because they just want to say they have played there. And unless you're booking more than six months in advance, it's hard to get in to play. "We form relationships with the artists," Bill says. "Sometimes if no one is playing, a guy will walk in with a guitar and ask if we mind if he plays a song. Maybe it turns out he's been coming for years and just wanted to play. Eventually, he becomes part of the circuit, and we have him back." That's the best way to perform at the Starlight: simply show up.

Diego agrees there's a definite mystery in the air at the Starlight. "There's something happening all the time," Diego says. "We never know what movie star is going to walk through the door. This place is full of magic. I can imagine in the mining days there would have been rows of movie theater chairs in here. I think a lot of that energy is maintained in this building."

The community comes together to celebrate and to mourn. The ghost town locals give off a spirit of both connectedness and solitude. The Dia de Los Muertos, or Day of the Dead, is an annual tradition where all are welcome.

"It has grown each year," Bill says. "More folks participate in it now, and the community turns it into what it is. It's a little bit different each year." Bill brings hundreds of tamales and candles to share, and the community brings dishes for a potluck dinner. "Musicians show up, kids come and decorate the cemetery and make it real beautiful," Bill says. "The entire school came from San Jacinto and the park [Big Bend

National Park] and so did the folks from the Terlingua school." The gathering takes place in the Ghost Town Cemetery on November 2 every year. "No matter what the weather is at sundown, that's when we gather," says Bill. Everyone is welcome at the celebration whether you know someone buried in the cemetery or not.

In a town with such a colorful tradition, ghost stories are strangely absent. "I'm probably the biggest ghost in ghost town because I come in at night, and no one sees me," Bill laughs.

Diego chimes in saying "I feel the spirit of it—not that I think there are ghosts—but I can feel a presence. Also, if the light bulb breaks you can blame it on them (the ghosts). I go to the Day of the Dead to personally visit some of my friends that have been buried there and pay respect. There are a few people who were very close to me there, so for me, it's an emotional thing. It's not a party scene. It's special in the way that it's set up and presented. Everyone is there in good spirits to remember their passed loved ones. People will bring pictures and flowers."

Just down the road from the cemetery and next door to the Starlight is the Terlingua Trading Company where you'll find cultural keepsakes, books, maps, chili seasoning, and other unique gifts from the region.

The High Sierra Bar and Grill at El Dorado Hotel is another popular watering hole that offers Tex-Mex, healthy salads, and hand-cut steaks as well as live music. You'll meet Deanna and Herman on their covered porch as you walk up to check in or as you check out. Deanna got involved with the chili community through Roger Foltz, a friend of High Sierra.

Chili eventually became her charity and Deanna now operates a 501(c)(3) called Ghost Town Charities. Through her chili cook-off in January, she hosts over one hundred cooks and raises money to help the community buy things such as propane, medical assistance, and basic needs for those who need a helping hand.

Espresso y Poco Mas operated by La Posada Milagro Guesthouse and Casitas serves coffee, smoothies, breakfast, fresh homemade salsa, and healthy lunches until about 2 p.m. In addition to keeping you fed, they have a beautiful guesthouse directly above the coffee shop, which has a cool outdoor community kitchen for guests and offers another great vantage point for killer views of the mountains and the ghost town.

Sit around the porch long enough and you'll meet Dr. Doug, a local icon who has inhabited the area since the '70s. His site *drdougs.com* describes his mental health clinic with

authentic Terlinguan humor:

"Just go through that door over there and the nurse will provide your favorite ice-cold medicine for a small fee. Come back here with your medicine and find a place on one of those benches. I'll guide you through this group therapy session, and I guarantee you will feel better very soon. Now tell me... What do you think of the view from this porch... Did you know Terlingua is the world's largest open air insane asylum? Yes, and I'm the only mental therapist in this entire borderland region, as far as the eye can see, when sitting on this mountain. This is a task no other therapist will do, a fate of unending hardships."

Dr. Doug goes on to give the following advice on his site: "Live free, take your medicine, and be very, very happy."

If the wind is right and you can find Internet service, search for a copy of the latest *Terlingua Moon* online for live music shows as well as community news and events. You can also tune in to KYOTE streaming radio along with about 500 other listeners to get the local scoop and hear songs like Alex Whitmore's "Alien Spaceship" or Jim Keaveny's "Ridin' Boots." Stop in at Long Draw Pizza for a great pizza (that's all they serve), and check out whatever else is open seasonally."

"Every day is a special story if you sit out here and watch the sunset behind the Chisos mountains," shares Diego. "It's a different color every day. It's a beautiful sight. The mountains turn purple and pink, and the sky has different kinds of clouds. I never get sick of taking pictures."

"People gather here [at the Starlight Theatre] on the porch and play music. It's the social network of Terlingua. Someone will show up with a guitar; someone will show up with a fiddle, and before you know it you have a picking circle. People come for the weekend; blow out a tire and never leave." Diego says one of the key members of his staff was once a broken-hearted harmonica player who chose to stay. "We keep a few instruments for anyone to pick up and play. The guitar stays on the porch overnight, and it's never been stolen. Anyone can pick it up and play it. It's amazing what can happen on that porch."

Thus describes part of the fabric of Terlingua, a place where you'll run into the most colorful people you'll find on the border chatting it up on the porch of a local hang-out, gathering together to view the most majestic sunsets Texas has to offer.

BIG BEND BUCKET LIST

From beautiful hikes and outdoor experiences to rustic dining opportunities and large festivals, the Big Bend region has much to offer seekers on a spiritual quest and travelers looking for adventures. Here is a revised excerpt from The Big Bend Cookbook with a bucket list of items you'll want to explore while visiting the Wild West. Following the bucket list, the chili cooks (also known as "chiliheads") hand out advice on how to stay entertained in the Big Bend region.

Alpine

Eat: Reata Restaurant, Saddle Club Alpine, La Casita, Plaine Coffee, Cow Dog

Stay: The Maverick Inn or Holland Hotel

Photo Ops: Twin Peaks mountains, "the desk" at Hancock Hill, murals in town

Indoors: Frontier Street Books,The Museum of the Big Bend at Sul Ross State University, and several art galleries

Outdoors: Hancock Hill

Nightlife: Railroad Blues, Saddle Club

Fort Davis
Eat: Poco Mexico, the Black Bear
Stay: Hotel Limpia, the Indian Lodge
Photo Ops: Ft. Davis Drug Store, Ft. Davis National Historic Site
Indoors: Chihuahuan Desert Research Institute, ample shopping ops
Outdoors: McDonald Observatory, Prude Ranch, Davis Mountains State Park, Balmorhea State Park-San Soloman Springs

Marfa/Valentine
Eat: Cochineal, Jett's Grill, Squeeze, Pizza Foundation, Planet Marfa, MarPho, Food Shark
Stay: Thunderbird Hotel, The Hotel Paisano, El Cosmico
Photo Ops: Prada Marfa, the water tower, Presidio Country Courthouse
Indoors: Several galleries, The Get Go, Big Bend Coffee Roasters, Marfa Book Company, The Well
Outdoors: Chinati Hot Springs (past Marfa)
Nightlife: Lost Horse, area hotels

Marathon
Eat: Marathon Coffee Shop, Johnny B's, 12 Gage at the Gage Hotel
Stay: Marathon Motel, Gage Hotel
Photo Ops: The Famous Burro
Indoors: James Evans Gallery
Outdoors: Post Park

Terlingua / Lajitas
Eat: Starlight Theatre, Long Draw Pizza, High Sierra Bar & Grill, Tivo's, Chili Pepper Café
Stay: Lajitas Golf Resort and Spa, El Dorado Hotel, La Posada Milagro Guesthouse and Casitas
Photo Ops: Ghost Town cemetery, Terlingua Trading Company, Starlight Theatre
Outdoors: Lajitas Golf Resort, Aguas Frias, the ghost town, adventure sports (rafting, horseback riding, etc.)

Big Bend National Park:
Hikes: the Window, the hot springs, the South Rim, there is so much to explore - do as much as you can.

More tips on enjoying Big Bend from the chili cooks:
"Be prepared to go remote. Bring water, an extra can of gas, some blankets, snacks, and a map of the area. Do not rely on your cell phone for directions, as reception is sketchy at best. Dress in layers and watch the weather." Mirt Foster

What are your favorite or most memorable meals from restaurants in the Big Bend area?

"When I worked in the park [Big Bend National Park], my girlfriend (now wife) and I would rush down [from the park] after shifts or on days off and would go on dates mostly to the Starlight. We loved the wide range of food and drinks on the menu. Also, La Kiva's BBQ was our favorite, and we loved hanging out there with friends. La Kiva will be open again soon. When I say soon, I mean Terlingua time soon. It will once again be one of our favorite spots!" Diego Palacios

"My favorite meals were chipotle pork chops at the Starlight and the Lajitas Fajitas when it was still owned by Walter Mischer." Jenny Turner

"Carolina White's homemade tamales at the Terlingua Store, the best Mexican food I've ever eaten. And a bowl of Miss Jenny's chili." Scott Turner

"There are many, but the tiny organic grocery in Fort Davis with its wide, breezy porch is a perfect spot to eat lunch and ponder your next adventure. Don't miss their daily home-made soups!" Mirt Foster

"We all love Nancy's at Long Draw Pizza in Terlingua. It's one of the best pizzas you'll ever eat in your life. You can walk around, and there are pictures and posters of all of the years of the chili cook-off she has managed to accumulate." Roger Foltz

Reata [in Alpine] ranked up there as one of the best eating experiences I've ever had." Barbara Collins

"Tivo's on South Highway 90 has the best chile rellenos I've ever tasted. In typical West Texas fashion, they have questionable hours of operation." Jennifer Boomer

"Beef tenderloin tamales at Reata and Magoo's Chile Macho." Maurine Winkley

"Green chili enchiladas at Alicia's in Alpine. Lamb chops at Maiya's in Marfa." Mark Hinshaw

"Cowboy dinner at the chili cook-off!" Matthew Walker

"Steak at the Starlight." Dwight Hamilton

What is your favorite activity to do while visiting Big Bend or a great memory you want to share?

"My favorite activity would have to be going on private river trips. We are so very fortunate we have friends that work the Rio Grande and still want to go on trips on their days off!" Diego Palacios

"Eat soft tacos al carbon with fresh guacamole at Chili Pepper Café." Jenny Turner

"See my mom and ride the river when there's water sloshing

on the banks." Scott Turner

"Well, the best agenda is no agenda, but generally, it's bird and people watching by day, star watching by night. A trip to the White Buffalo Bar is a must. Last year we watched the Academy Awards in Marathon. Richard Linklater's nominated film, "Boyhood" was filmed in part at nearby Sul Ross University in Alpine." Mirt Foster

"Take photos!" Jennifer Boomer

"I go to Boquillas, and I go to Presidio every time. I like the canyons and driving that route from Terlingua to Presidio. I like the ghost town and the mine. I like to see the sunset on the mountains. I get up early and go to the graveyard when the sun starts to rise; that's a cool scene. I go to Big Bend National Park—just to see the same views every year. I like to hike and walk through the park and look through the rocks." Tom Dozier

"Balmorhea, Marathon, hike the South Rim. Then eat in Terlingua and find a place to camp out. Check out the Marfa lights, go for a drive. Pick any road and it's awesome." Maurine Winkley

"We had an opportunity with 2-Alarm to have some photos made of Gordon and me. We normally went [to Terlingua] in November for the cook-off, but this time, we went out in April. This was back in the '80s, and you didn't have all the hotels or as many people. We went out for a photo session, and the cacti were in bloom, bright with color. Cactus in the spring gives tremendous color. We were up before daylight for hiking—that was very enjoyable.

"During that photo shoot, we got the idea to shoot a 2-Alarm movie in Luckenbach, which we shot on an eight-millimeter camera. The language was so bad that we decided we couldn't put it out to our friends and the public, so we made it a silent movie. Then we had a caption contest. We held a world pre-miere at the chili shop at Fourth and Brazos. We showed it as a black tie affair and served champagne and popcorn. There was a limo out front, and we would take pictures of people as if they had arrived in the limo. That idea came from that photo session we did in Terlingua. There are always photo ops out there, November or any other time of year." Tom Nall

"Road bike riding, hiking, and canoeing down the Rio Grande." Mark Hinshaw

"Relaxing." Matthew Walker

If you could send someone on a tour of the Big Bend region for a week, where would you tell them to go and what would you suggest they do?

"I would recommend hikes in Big Bend National Park and Big Bend State Park. The trails are spectacular and well worth the effort! Definitely a river trip with Big Bend River Tours or Desert Sports. My personal favorite is a three-day Santa Elena Canyon trip. But I'll hop on any trip; they are all glorious. I would also recommend Desert Sports for guided mountain biking trips through the desert. You can always hook up with one of our horseback riding outfits. All these activities are really special. And, of course, after what will be a wonderful day, come to the Starlight for a great meal,

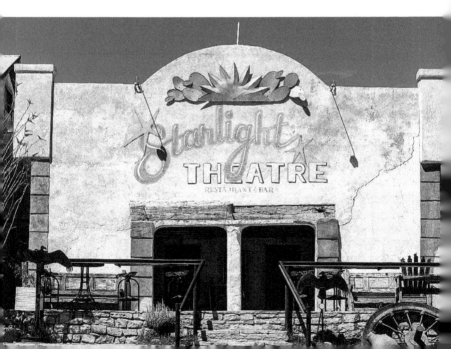

drinks, and live entertainment. Music and art also play a huge role in our community. Some nights you will find a ten-piece dance band, many gifted locals playing during dinner, or at any given time day or night, someone or everyone will be playing on the porch. For memorabilia trinkets or gifts, don't miss the Terlingua Trading Company right next door." Diego Palacios

"Go on a river trip if the water is high enough (and spend at least two nights on the river to really experience it), hike to the top of Lost Mine Trail, pack your passport and visit Boquillas, Mexico. Have a cold drink and watch the sunset from the ghost town porch [Starlight Theatre]." Jenny Turner

"Since it takes forever to get there from just about anywhere, an early start is a good idea. I would stop in Balmorhea Springs for a cool swim then head to Fort Davis. Stay the night and drive up to the McDonald Observatory for a Star Party. The next day is Marfa and the art galleries, a late lunch in Alpine, then on to Marathon and the refuge of the Gage Hotel—a perfect jumping off point for the next day's drive into Big Bend National Park and the towns of Terlingua, Lajitas, etc." Mirt Foster

"Always the first place is up in the [Chisos] Basin [at Big Bend National Park]. That's the first place I went to when I was five years old. All the old buildings that were old white buildings, that's where I stayed as a child. Other years we stayed in the rock cabins; number four faces the Window. When I bring friends there, we reminisce and see those rocks where I used to climb. I have great memories of the basin. My husband's mother would care for my sons Patrick and Steven while we were busy at the cook-off. Both boys have been going most of their lives." Kathleen Tolbert Ryan

"I would highly recommend seeing a movie in the theater in Alpine because it's an old-time movie theater. Stay at the Gage in Marathon; it's only thirty miles from Alpine. Alpine and Marathon impressed me with things to see. Even though the trains are loud, the rumbling of them going by is really nice." Barbara Collins

"Come hang out with me for a week, keep the hours that I keep, bring a spare liver, and hang out with my friends. Since I'm a [CASI] director, I get there Saturday [before the cook-off] ready to work and I work all week. I'm on the ranch one hundred percent of the time. You can come hang out with me, and you'll have a kick-ass time and a bunch of stories to tell people. I can take you to some breathtaking views on the CASI ranch, but I've never done the area tour." Kris Hudspeth

"Rafting the Rio Grande is the most memorable activity. Hiking Mule Ears Peaks. One time going down with Mom and Dad, a friend of mine, a sister and her friend, we went into the town of Terlingua to the bar. At night, three cowboys came in riding horseback, and one was a lady. They were gun-holstering cowboys in the town square; it was like being in the Wild, Wild West. They called themselves the Eagles: Black Eagle, Lady Hawk and another name I can't recall. It was the last of the Wild, Wild West. They put their horses up at the tie-off, walked in the bar, and had drinks. I was probably fourteen at the time. In Terlingua—thirty-six years ago." Debbie Webb

"Cruise Pinto Canyon Road, the Fort Davis Loop, and the River Road. Eat in Marfa. Catch a Doodlin' Hogwallops concert. Drink beer in the afternoon on the Terlingua porch with all the colorful locals. Stay the night at Chinati Hot Springs. Hire me to tag along and take photos of your entire Big Bend adventure." Jennifer Boomer

"Go to the hot springs. Attend the chili cook-off. Look at the stars. Get drunk at La Kiva. Visit the Stillwater Museum." Wally Roberts

"Relax, visit the parks, drink plenty of water." Richard Willis

"Get there a couple of days earlier and visit the area. There's so much to do outside the cook-off. People drive over there and never leave the ranch where the cook-off takes place. There are plenty of people who get down there and stay at the ranch all week. But my advice is to get down there earlier and enjoy the area." Tom Dozier

"Go horseback riding, take a river trip, take advantage of

photo ops even with your phone, cross the border at Boquillas. I've taken my family across to Boquillas. I hadn't been there in years, and I was amazed that people remembered me. The oarsman said, 'Tomas!' I used to take clothes over there across the river to donate. Those people remembered that and everywhere I went, people were calling me by my name. Boquillas is always a highlight. You have to have a passport to get across the river because of 9/11. It was shut down after 9/11, and they just reopened it a year or so ago. Take the rowboat across and ride donkeys up to the town. They have two to three cantinas—great food, tacos, cold beer, tequila. I can remember Gordon and his wife, and me and my wife—we went down to the mayor's house just below the town dump one trip. He asked us down for dinner. I remember the floor was a dirt floor in their little casa. My wife said 'I've never seen such a collection of Tupperware anywhere in my life.' Boquillas is a wonderful trip; it can be a highlight of your trip." Tom Nall

"I am into telescopes, and this is the best place in the nation for dark skies, so that is something I recommend to anyone." Charlie Throop

"Visit both parks (the national park and the state park). Both are so different and unique in their own way. I love the state park drive and eating in the basin. Go to the river company outfits and take a float on the river." Deanna Castillo

"Hike the South Rim at BBNP [Big Bend National Park].

Have a drink at La Kiva, bring a jacket and check out Star Party at McDonald Observatory. Bring your passport and go to Boquillas. Take a dip at Balmorhea. Check out the great beers at Big Bend Brewing—ahem." Mark Hinshaw

"Lajitas: go zip-lining. Stop at La Kiva for a drink. The scenery speaks for itself, so there is nothing more to say." Matthew Walker

"I'd send them during the first weekend of November and tell them to go to the cook-off." Dwight Hamilton

What advice would you give someone attending the cook-off for the first time as a competitor and a visitor?

"Wear yer boots, hat, bring a cooler, and your best chili game!" Mirt Foster

"Park your RV on level ground, away from drunks parked up the hill from you in a giant brown pickup truck. Enough said." Scott Turner

"If you are planning to drink, find a comfortable spot and stay there. It's best just to stay off the roads that weekend!" Jenny Turner

"Relax, ask for help, take an active part." Richard Willis

"Meet as many people as you can; the people that you hear about or see in the paper or see on the chili trails. Spend that time with them. People will give you that time and share their information. They are willing to talk with you. I always think that when you go out there the first time, it's overwhelming because people tend to think they need to change their chili to match the area. But no—you cook what you cook best. If you cook a hotter chili, keep it—don't change nothing because you're going to a different town. You were qualified to go. That means you are among the best. So cook what you cook best, don't change anything. People tend to change their recipe up—the heat of their chili, just cook what you cook best." Tom Dozier

"My first time going was in 2015. It was cool knowing that there are multiple camps and understanding the nuances of each. I definitely wasn't expecting all the chili to have to be made the same way at CASI. Being able to differentiate your chili but using the same protocol as everyone else is special, and I tasted a lot of wonderful pots of chili out there. My advice is to go to both cook-offs. Check them both out and try as much as you can. It's good because everyone gives you little sample cups and you can taste a lot of them." Maurine Winkley

"Bring as much stuff as you can, and don't get on the roads if you have been drinking." Charlie Throop

"Wear a big hat, and be ready for anything." Mark Hinshaw

"Be prepared for the sun. Drink lots of water. If you compete, make sure your chili tastes good cold. By the time it gets to the last judge, it will be cold." Matthew Walker

"Have fun and watch the speed limit." Dwight Hamilton

"Wish I had time for just one more bowl of chili."

—Alleged dying words of Kit Carson (1809–1868), frontiersman and mountain man

"Chili is much improved by having had a day to contemplate its fate."

—John Steele Gordon, writer

"Chili is not so much food as a state of mind. Addictions to it are formed early in life, and the victims never recover. On blue days in October, I get this passionate yearning for a bowl of chili, and I nearly lose my mind."

—Margaret Cousins (1905–1996), novelist

THE TERLINGUA CHILI COOK-OFF

The Terlingua chili story starts in 1967 on property owned by racecar driver Carroll Shelby and David Witts, an attorney. With the intention of stimulating the sale of the land as well as promoting Frank X. Tolbert's book, *A Bowl of Red,* Tolbert and Tom Tierney (public relations for Ford Motor Company) developed the cook-off concept and pitted Wick Fowler against Dave Chasen. Chasen grew ill and was replaced by author H. Allen Smith.

That first year drew plenty of attention in media across the nation. Hallie Stilwell, Floyd Schneider, and Dave Witts judged the event. Hallie voted for H. Allen, Floyd voted for Wick, and Dave spat out both chili samples, claiming the ruination of his taste buds. Subsequently, that first year was a draw. In a signature spirit of mischief that pervaded future cook-offs, the ballot box was stolen during the second year's competition and thrown into a mineshaft.

The cook-off which began as a spoof and promotion to sell Carroll Shelby's property has grown into what he once called an "adult Woodstock" and has continued an unexpected fifty years. "It was just fun between writers," shares Gordon

Fowler. "My dad (Wick) challenged H. Allen Smith, and it was just meant for fun. After the second year, Dad said, 'It's done. It was a great promotion, but it's over.' Little did he know it was going to go on forever."

The original cook-off was managed under one umbrella in Terlingua from 1967 through 1974. Besides, the chili cook-off, the early days saw quirky competitions outside of the chili tents, like the armadillo races put on by Jalapeno Sam Lewis. In 1975, Shelby's group left and formed the International Chili Society (ICS) based in California. From 1975 to 1982, the two groups co-existed, each holding their version of the world chili championship. But in 1983, the Terlingua group split in two. "To cook at Terlingua, a person must qualify by earning sufficient points at local competitions during the chili year. Even more confusing is that two Terlingua championships take place on the same day every year due to a split in the chili religion back in 1983," shares chili judge Richard Willis.

Both Tolbert's group and the Chili Appreciation Society International (CASI) group continue to host their world championships the first Saturday of November in Terlingua just six miles apart. Tolbert's has more of an old cowboy reunion feel to it complete with teepees and covered wagons. The CASI vibe is both more structured and a little wilder. The CASI site has presentation stages and a permanent judging area. It also includes the Old 320 area for the cooking (which gives a nod to the 320 people who invested in the land sold by Shelby and Witt) and Krazy Flats for the spectators.

In short, the original cook-off has split into three different chili-cooking organizations: Tolbert's Behind the Store, Chili Appreciation Society International (CASI) and the International Chili Society (ICS). Each has their own rules and guidelines and different operating procedures, but at the end of the day, they are all cooking chili for charity and for braggin' rights.

GORDON FOWLER

"What I like about chili is that everybody does it differently," Gordon tells me over the phone during one of our conversations. "CASI has a lot of rules. In the old days, it was just characters making chili their way, and it was interesting—but I'm thinking like an artist instead of a chili guy."

Gordon first learned of the Terlingua chili cook-off while in combat during Vietnam. "I was a first marine division combat correspondent with a capital 'C' on combat," Gordon tells me. Consequently, he was wounded several times, "but I made it through," he says. "I was sitting around with marine infantry guys about to go on a sweep. One of them got a copy of *Stars and Stripes*. This guy says, 'Fowler, is this your dad?' I said, 'What are you talking about?' And there on the front page of *Stars and Stripes* was news about the world champion cook-off. *Stars and Stripes* had an enormous circulation in the military at that time. It was like the *New York Times* of the military. Since I was a correspondent for them [*Stars and Stripes*], the Marines teased me about it; that's what Marines do. It's kind of surreal to be sitting in a foxhole, and your dad's on the front page of the paper."

His sister wrote him later after the cook-off explaining the event in Terlingua. She sent clippings from all the papers. It had made the front page of the *New York Times*, several Texas papers including the *Dallas Morning News*, and more. "We didn't have the communications we have now," says Gordon. He goes on to say that in the hospital after he was wounded, patients were only allowed one telephone call. "Even then we had to wait in line for hours," he remembers. "We might get one call in thirteen months, and if you didn't write to people, no one would write you."

Gordon makes his chili with the 2-Alarm seasonings (from his father Wick's company), meat, and fresh garlic and onions. "I do it by eyeball," he shares. "We started the 2-Alarm chili company inspired by my grandmother's basic recipe. My dad loved the way his mother-in-law from Gonzales made chili. Most people knew how to make it [chili] in the early days," he says referring to the traditional meat and spice ingredients.

"Dad formed the Chili Appreciation Society International [chapter of CASI] in Dallas," Gordon shares. "He was a pretty famous workhorse. He could get a job with a newspaper anytime and go back and forth. He was also a chef and wanted to make chili [a spice mixture] for friends and put it in little bags so they could make it. He told my sister and me about the idea, and we thought it sounded rather labor intensive." But despite their skepticism, Gordon says they made 150 bags of the 2-Alarm Chili Kit. "We looked like drug dealers," he laughs about that first round, "filling these little sacks and putting them on the scale. Connie Hernandez was our first employee. She and I and my first wife sent them out to friends. Within two weeks we had orders for over two thousand packages."

Gordon says the only other product in those days was Chili Quick. "It cost eighteen cents at the grocery store and made the world's shittiest chili," he says. "So ours was good. Normal people in cities that didn't grow up with that South Texas influence didn't know how to make it. It [the 2-Alarm Chili Kit] was good, and there was nothing like it anywhere.

"We got all these orders and were swamped," Gordon continues. "We had to get more help to fill the bags. Wick left me in charge. I had lost my job because I had gotten drafted, so I packed a bunch of chili in the back of his car (mine had been totaled by a drunk). I linked up with Minor Wilson in Houston along with Jerry Jeff Walker and Townes Van Zandt." Gordon says he would sell enough chili out of the trunk of the car to make between ten and twenty dollars a day. During this time, he says he lived on Minor's couch. "Every night we'd get with Guy Clark, Jerry Jeff, and the guys. In those years, Guy wrote 'LA Freeway,' Jerry recorded it, and it hit the charts. Townes went on to Nashville. Guy and Minor had a guitar shop for a while, but they broke it up because they weren't selling anything. Guy went to Nashville, and Minor and his wife went to San Francisco following Janis Joplin out there. There was a whole contingent of Texans living on Beaver Street out there too. Jerry Jeff came to Austin and about that time. He and my wife and Willie Nelson started the great progressive country music scare of 1970.

"All the chili and music were all intertwined," Gordon continues. "I was cooking chili down there; they were always smoking pot, so they were always hungry. Jerry Jeff was from New Jersey, and he was down here trying to act like a Texan. So we were trying to teach him how to talk. He considers himself a Texan [now], and he's been here a long time. So I guess it stuck.

"When the company (2-Alarm) first started, I went to Vietnam. Dad was still alive, so I didn't get involved. But he died in 1972. I was at a dead-end job as an art director for a magazine. I borrowed five thousand dollars from Mike Mays loaned on a signature with no collateral and found Tom Nall (he was a chili cook-off guy that was selling me insurance). I told him, 'If you can sell insurance, I bet you can sell the hell out of chili.' I brought him to work at a cheap salary because we weren't making money at that point. He took a chance on it and moved his young wife down here. We did $50,000 in sales the first year and $360,000 in sales the second year, and then we hit one million. Everyone in the world wanted to buy me [2-Alarm] after that."

At the time, Gordon knew Kit Goldsbury of Pace Picante. "He was a son-in-law of the Paces who ended up buying the company and taking it up to over one billion," Gordon shares. "We were going to trade stock back when we were both small. He wanted ten percent of my company, and we would get one to two percent of his. If I had taken it, two percent of one billion would have been worth it." Gordon smiles. "I did fine anyway," he says.

Eventually, he did sell the company, and in his words, "It's doing fine." The new company would still send spices to his sister Ann while she was still alive. "She [Ann] was the most creative writer of any of us," Gordon recalls, "but we couldn't get her to do it beyond her letters. One time she wrote Victor Borge, a famous comic and piano player, and he wrote her back. So, they wrote for ten years. She also wrote the actors that became chili fans. She wrote thousands of letters to people who ordered our chili by mail and developed this enormous mail order business because she liked to do that. It took a lot off of me," he confesses. "I'm bad about that."

In addition to the chili company, Gordon has always been an artist. "As a kid, I always did the posters for school and everything." He says he visited a lot of museums when he was young. Whenever a new exhibit opened in San Antonio or Austin, his mom would take him to see it. "So I had a taste for it [art] from second grade on," he says.

"When I was in the war they knew I liked art, but I was a writer," says Gordon. He was assigned to bodyguard a gentleman from the *Saturday Evening Post,* who was a friend of Norman Rockwell. "I would take him around and sketch wherever we were. He told me to go to art school and that he thought I would do really well. So, when I came home I started doing it, but I had other things interfering—like work.

"I built a studio in the chili office," shares Gordon. "Every moment I got a chance to do a workshop, I'd study a week with different teachers. I'm just going to paint until I drop, cook chili now and then, and play a little music."

TOM NALL

"I had read about the chili cook-off in the *Dallas Morning News*," Tom Nall shares about his learning of the Terlingua cook-off. "Frank X. Tolbert wrote a regular article called "Tolbert's Texas." It was a fun article about different things going on in Texas. My roommate and I had read his article, and we decided to make that journey. We didn't even know where Terlingua was before that article, but we went. We stayed at an adobe hut that was just three walls and no roof. It was nothing but a party down there. Chili cooking was just an excuse to be there and to party.

"I felt like I'd known those people [in Terlingua] all my life. From that first trip around 1972, I have some of my best friends that I have to this day. Bob Wilson was my roommate, and we decided we needed to get into this chili cooking business. One year we won more cook-offs in Texas than any other chili team. That's how I met the Fowlers: Wick, Ann, Gordon. They were fun-loving, and again chili was just an excuse to get together. People didn't take it near as serious in those early days, and everyone was just out having a good time. I know there were cook-offs and winners were decided, but not much judging really took place.

"One year this guy came out and cooked in the cook-off but didn't win. He asked, 'Why did you pick so and so to win? Why did you pick *him*?' Gordon (Fowler) said: 'Well, we just liked him so much more than we liked you,' and that was the truth." Tom says that choosing a winner didn't necessarily mean choosing the best tasting chili in those days. He says he doesn't even remember if Gordon was judging that year. "It goes to show we were just there to have a good time.

"Chili is just a reason to get people together and have fun." It's the same reason Tom likes tequila. He says it's all about having a good time whether it's about making margaritas, sipping the tequila, or slamming shots. "It's just having fun. Chili is the same way," he says. "It's a fun, fun food. Everyone has his or her favorite recipes and spice mix preferences: 2-Alarm, 1-Alarm, False-alarm; it's just fun to cook. There are so many different stories on how chili was invented and I always like the phrase: There's always the truth, and there's always a myth, and the myth is usually more fun."

Tom hauled horses down to Terlingua for a number of years. "We had a horse drawn chuckwagon we drove around the cook-off site," he shares. "A lot of our friends started riding, so we trailered part of the way and rode up in the basin.

One year, Tom brought along Sidekick, a 16-year old young man that Tom was mentoring, and they rode from Alpine to Terlingua. They were riding to raise money for ALS—the disease that had taken Wick Fowler's life. "We've raised an awful lot of money for people who fight that disease," Tom says. "I told Sidekick we should ride and see how much money we could raise. When it came time I asked him, 'Are we gonna make that ride?' He said, 'Are you serious?' I said, 'Yes, we gave folks our word on stage.' So we went. We slept on the ground each night. It took us three days, and we raised seventy thousand dollars in donations. We rode into camp like they did the old cowboy way. I've got great pics of that. We rode into Terlingua at 5:30 p.m. Everybody had lined up down the road—makes me teary-eyed to think about it. It was quite an accomplishment."

Two years later they had ten riders start, and eight of them finished. "We did the same format—spent the night along the way, ate lunch along the road. We had a support group to help us with food and make sure the horses were ok. We knew we were going to end up in Terlingua, but one of the ranchers locked the gates, and we couldn't get through. One of the girls got bucked off, and someone in a jeep had to get her out. We raised another seventy thousand dollars during that ride."

Tom tells of another sort of a ride he did to raise money for chili charity. "We drove the chuckwagon from Austin to San Antonio and stopped at a Walmart asking for donations. That took a week, and we made about twenty thousand dollars. We have done that a few times. There is still no cure. If you're diagnosed with ALS, you're going to die. But ALS has become the charity of choice.

"Terlingua has become what we call a party with a purpose. We are fighting that disease. Again, this all occurred because of Wick Fowler's untimely death of ALS, and the fact that he was one of the founders of the cook-off."

Tom recalls when he first got into the Fowler's family business. "I was selling insurance. I was down in Houston and had taken my LSAT and [was] interviewing with schools to go to law school. I got a call from Gordon and Ann Fowler; Wick had recently died." They had inherited the company when Wick died and wanted to discuss insurance policies. "I was in Houston, so I drove to Austin the next day, and we visited about their insurance. We got on motorcycles and rode out to The Pier, an old restaurant on Lake Austin. I had ridden horses, bulls, broncs, but never a motorcycle. I wasn't afraid, but I wasn't real smart either," he laughs. "We sat around and visited down at The Pier, and I drove back to Dallas on a Thursday. Friday, I got a call. Gordon asked if I'd visit with him about going to work for 2-Alarm in marketing and sales. I told him I didn't know about the grocery business, and he said, 'We don't either.' I went there Monday to interview. In 1975, we landed in Austin and remained there 'til this day.

"My mother and father got married on December 6, 1941, and lived in Texas all their life. My mother had never been out of Dallas County. But the day after they were married, Pearl Harbor was bombed." Tom's father was called up to report to a torpedo yard in Washington D.C. They moved there the following week and Tom was born during their stay. "We moved back to Texas when the war was over. So, I consider myself a misplaced Texan. It's like those bumper stickers say, 'I wasn't born here, but I got here as soon as I could.'

"I've been real lucky. Who in the world could imagine being in the chili business for thirty-two years and then retiring? That [retirement] lasted two days before I went into the tequila business. I have to say a lot of that was good fortune and luck. I taught school, I coached, I sold insurance. 2-Alarm was sold a couple of times, but I was always fortunate to stay with the company." He says once he got together with some other people in management and tried to buy the company back from Proctor and Gamble. Proctor and Gamble, however, reneged on their promise of the first right of refusal to Tom and his co-workers. He continued to work for the company after Reily Foods in New Orleans purchased it. But things had changed from when Gordon, Ann and Shorty Fry worked at the company.

"Gordon and I hired Shorty Fry, and she worked for 2-Alarm for seventeen years. We bought a guest ranch in Colorado in 1995, and she went up to be a ranch foreman. She's still there today, and she's seventy-eight. She's a character," Tom says. "I was a bull rider, and the last ride I did she was a rodeo clown. She was big in the chili cook-off. She didn't have a flourishing figure, so in the spirit of fun, she put on a low neck t-shirt, and we would get a Marks-A-Lot [permanent marker] and marked the word "front" below her neck as a joke, so other folks would know she was a woman. She would wear it all through the cook-off."

Tom remembers another Shorty story: "We were all cold standing around a fire at Luckenbach. Everyone was outside around the potbellied stove, and Shorty said 'Tom, I'm gonna streak the store at 8 p.m. tonight—don't tell anyone.' I said, 'Ok, you know I won't.' I saw she was outside about five minutes 'til eight, so I went on and told everyone, and we all went out the other door," he laughs. "No one wanted to see her that way," Tom says kindheartedly of his friend.

"2-Alarm has been very, very good to me. It was a tremendously fun ride, and I'm very proud of what we accomplished," he says referring to building the company from a small mail order business into a nationally recognized grocery store brand. Tom says that though none of them were MBAs—they ran the business the way they believed was best, which brought a breath fresh air to the grocery industry at that time. "It wasn't all just luck, though," Tom says. "I've worked hard too. But that's just part of my DNA. It's the way my momma and daddy raised me; that's what you do.

"One of the first gentlemen I met out there in Terlingua was Chris Regas. There's a cowboy camp we created fifteen years ago, and we would have a dinner every Friday night. He's a portrait photographer, now eighty-nine years old. I met him when he was probably forty. He now suffers from Alzheimer's, so to honor him on his seventieth birthday, we started having this dinner in Terlingua to raise money for Lou Gehrig's disease." Tom was preparing to visit him when we talked. "I'll see him next week and hope he remembers me. If

he does, he smiles and we hug each other. That's the kind of friendships we have developed over the years. It's amazing that they all came about because of the chili cook-off. I met

Jani [Allegani Jani Schofield] the year she won the cook-off. She's special. We have been friends ever since. Kathleen Ryan was seventeen years old when I first met her at Terlingua. It's amazing. It's a great group of people.

"When people go out there for the first time, you will feel like you've known these people for your whole life. All the decorations fall away; you just go out to have a good time, and be yourself, and not everybody does that every day."

KATHLEEN TOLBERT RYAN

Kathleen and her husband are directors for the Original International Frank X. Tolbert - Wick Fowler Championship Chili Cook-off. "I've only missed one when my son was born in November of 1986," says Kathleen. "We help run the cook-off, but there are a lot of volunteers that put it on.

"My dad (Frank X. Tolbert) and Tom Tierney and Carroll Shelby and David Witts: it was their idea. My dad was one of the founding fathers of the cook-off in the beginning. In his mind (and there are many different versions), but Tom Tierney was a public relations man in Dallas that was trying to promote Dad's book *A Bowl of Red*.

Together they thought of the idea of having a chili cook-off in the most remote place. Carroll Shelby and David Witts owned a lot of land in the ghost town, and that's why they chose that area to begin with. His

dear friend Wick Fowler was also a newspaper man, and he agreed to cook, and Hallie Stilwell agreed to judge."

No historical account of West Texas lore is complete without mentioning Hallie

Stillwell. A pioneer herself, Stillwell served as justice of the peace for nearly twenty years in Alpine. She was introduced to her first bowl of chili as a new bride on the Stillwell Ranch in 1918; she would have been twenty-one at the time. "You can imagine the shock I had when my husband Roy served me a bowl of chili. It was so hot with pepper that I couldn't eat it," she shared in Frank X. Tolbert's book *A Bowl of Red.*

Hallie developed a friendship with Frank Tolbert, a columnist in Dallas who would call her to verify news during her justice of the peace years. Tolbert published his chili recipe, but H. Allen Smith, a critic from New York well known for writing his own book on the subject: *The Great Chili Confrontation*, challenged him to a cook-off. As the story goes, Tolbert asked Wick, chief cook of the Chili Appreciation Society International of Dallas, to cook at the challenge which was to take place in Terlingua on the first weekend in November of 1967.

In an excerpt from the Tolbert's *A Bowl of Red,* Hallie recalls her experience as a judge for the very first cook-off: "I was asked to be a judge at the confrontation, along with Floyd Schneider, vice-president of a San Antonio brewery. We were blindfolded to sample the chili. My vote was cast; it went to Smith's chili. Schneider cast his vote for Fowler's chili. David Witt, the mayor of Terlingua, was the final judge, so he had to break the tie. He sampled one portion and choked. He tried some of the concoction from the other pot and spat it out. 'My taste buds are paralyzed,' he gasped. He declared the contest a tie and scheduled another confrontation for the next year."

Kathleen Tolbert Ryan is a fifth generation Texan. "We have had Tolbert's Restaurant since 1976. My youngest son Steven is a key player. He has taken over the music; he's a manager at age twenty-six, and he loves it. I love it. I've been in it since I was twenty-four."

Kathleen has been going to the cook-off in Terlingua since she was eighteen, but her first memory is driving up the hill to the basin when she was five with her dad. "My dad wrote for the *Dallas Morning News* (his column was "Tolbert's Texas") for thirty-seven years," she says. "Before that, he wrote for different newspapers. He had lost his father when he was twelve or thirteen and had read all of his books. He was the oldest of three boys and became a sports writer for the *Fort Worth Star-Telegram* before World War II. It was a great childhood traveling around Texas. He did the perimeter of Texas in a jeep with my brother sixty years ago. The *Dallas Morning News* provided a jeep for him. I have so much memorabilia here in Grapevine: all my dad's writings, letters from Carroll Shelby and H.L. Mencken and Stanley Marcus.

"Over the years, people were interested in making the cook-off more organized and less fun, and that's the reason it split," Kathleen shares with me. "My dad was into the original way it started: no points, no rules, just getting together to enhance the dish of chili, which eventually became the Texas state dish because of all of that."

The split happened in 1983 over disagreements on how to manage the cook-off. "It was an angry thing in a way," Kathleen shares with a sympathetic heart, "because we had a piece of property near Saw Mill Canyon." She says they

were planning to move the Tolbert cook-off there, but the opposing chili faction bulldozed the area and sent her dad threatening letters. "But all that is over, and we are friends with the other cook-off now." She says that sharing Terlingua with another chili cook-off is just fine. She is proud that both groups raise so much money for charity. "Our main charity is ALS/Lou Gehrig's disease," Kathleen says. "It's become a cook-off with a cause.

"The original people still come to our cook-off. That's why we call it the original. We are laid back," Kathleen shares. "There's no wet t-shirt contests anymore. We are more family-oriented but not all that innocent. We have this wonderful dinner Friday before the main cook-off. Tom Nall brings a chuckwagon and everyone brings a dish. Tolbert's Restaurant brings chili, and other people bring other dishes. Chris [Regas] would have a birthday celebration during the gathering. He would bring lamb, dolmas—quite a gourmet feast." Kathleen says that Tom would say a prayer, and then donations would be collected before going through the cooks' line for food. "It's an emotional event and a wonderful gathering.

"My oldest son Patrick is interested in the cook-off, where the younger son is more interested in the restaurant. Patrick has brought people from Texas Tech. They are bringing young people, and we are experiencing a changing of the guard and revitalization of the cook-off in some ways."

Many magazines have recognized Tolbert's Restaurant over the years. The acclaimed *Bon Appetit* magazine even listed the eatery as one of the best places to get chili. Kathleen says that her dad and brother developed the recipe used in the restaurant. "They use really great fresh spices and high-quality meat that is chuck tender and cut specifically. We use the same recipe as we did in '76, but we don't add a Lone Star beer anymore."

Regarding beans, Kathleen says that her dad's philosophy was not to cook the chili and beans together. "It just doesn't work out," she says. "He was not into having beans in chili. At Tolbert's we have 'north of the border.' If people want beans, we add it later."

A fifty-year lifespan for a cook-off is an amazing feat. "There's such a lot to tell," Kathleen continues. She says the first year all the men were like characters from the television series *Mad Men.* She remembers "big business men in their fifties, who drank whiskey. It was like their second childhood. They didn't really want women there, but they had Swedish women there. So, my mother chartered an airplane to drop flyers on the men telling them in protest that the women should be allowed to go. Hallie was the only woman besides the Swedish women. I became great friends with her, and she became our chili queen.

"Hallie was always there when my dad was alive and would always go to the cook-off. My brother and I would make her various crowns. There are several posters of her with our crown on her head. She and her daughter would show up even when she was in her nineties. She would get up on the stage and greet the group. She was really into going every year and signing her book *I'll Gather My Geese*. She was just like my grandmother. I named one of my dogs Hallie, and I don't know if she liked that or not," Kathleen jokes. "She had a lot of children named after her because she was such a wonderful person. It was sad that we lost her. She died a month before she turned one hundred."

Attendance at Tolbert's Behind the Store Cook-Off varies every year. "We are not about numbers," she says, "but we are about the quality of the festival. We may have 2,000 come. In some of the early years, there are photographs that show 5,000 to 10,000. Then the split happened, and it got divided up. The CASI cook-off has a lot more now. They are jammed in like sardines over there."

Both cook-offs fall on the same weekend. "In 1988, there was a lawsuit going," Kathleen remembers. "We had to go to Pecos for trial, and we lost our name CASI, which we shouldn't have. I try not to dwell on some of the bad things. The judge in Pecos was known as a character: he had a water gun he would spray people with. He said that we were splitting the baby in half like the Bible story. Some of my dad's friends and neighbors even testified against us." So, Kathleen and company continue to hold their cook-off on a large plot of land on the left of town as you enter Terlingua under a sign that proclaims "Behind the Store." But the store doesn't actually exist anymore, so the sign is the easiest way to identify the location. This is how the Tolbert faction came to be known as "Tolbert's Behind the Store." The CASI group continues to hold their cook-off separately at their private ranch a few miles further down the road.

Kathleen loves the area so much that she and her husband bought twenty acres and are building a house in Terlingua. "Financially, it's a good place to retire," she says. "We just love the area."

ROGER FOLTZ

Only two men to date have placed at the CASI cook-off and the Tolbert's cook-off on the same day: Roger Foltz and John Billy Murray. So I got on the phone with Roger Foltz to get another perspective on the chili lore.

"There are three chili religions," he tells me, "(1) Tolbert's, (2) CASI, and (3) ICS. All of us started at the same place at the same time," Roger says, referring to that first cook-off in 1967. In the early days, all three groups operated under one event. But eventually, Carroll Shelby broke away to form ICS and took his group to California. "In court, ICS has the right to call their cook-off the world championship," Roger denotes. "CASI calls theirs the International Chili Championship and Tolbert's calls theirs the Original International Chili Championship."

Each of the "religions" has their own point system by which competitors must accrue points at various cook-offs throughout the year. When the appropriate number of points is reached, they are invited to cook in their group's world championship.

Roger says people continue to cook chili even after they are qualified so they can continue to raise money for charity. "CASI, for example, will sponsor 550 cook-offs and raise over $1.5 million for various charities in a year," Roger offers. "Every cook-off associated with CASI has to have a charity tie-in. We have one that awards a scholarship to the Terlingua [Big Bend High School] valedictorian, and then virtually every other graduating student gets some kind of CASI help. All across the United States, we give various scholarships based on the amount of money we have allocated for the scholarship fund. Sometimes, we have enough to give a full ride."

CASI assigns different points to different states based on the number of cook-offs each state has in one year. There are six-point, nine-point, and twelve-point states. Texas is a twelve-point state, meaning a competitor must have twelve points to qualify to receive an invitation to the CASI International Championship. Competitors ranked in the top ten receive points based on their placement. First place receives four points, second place receives three points, and third place receives two points. Fourth through tenth place competitors receive one point each. A participant can qualify for the CASI world championship cook-off by winning three competitions in Texas—three first place wins equal 12 points total qualifying the competitor for the CASI cook-off in Terlingua.

CASI posts a judging sheet on their website that says, "Fine chili should look good, smell good, and taste good! Accordingly, each cup of chili is to be judged on five criteria to arrive at a whole number score of 1 to 10, with 10 being the highest. The five criteria are aroma, red color, consistency, taste, and aftertaste."

Judges evaluate the taste of chili in two ways: (1) the flavor that stands out when you first put the chili in your mouth, and (2) the aftertaste otherwise known as the "back heat" to chiliheads. "Back heat is the heat rising in your palate at the end," Roger helps clarify. "Everything is subjective. We want your personal opinion when you're judging."

Roger says that you can use any ground spices you want, but no fresh vegetables. "What the judges want to see is meat and gravy: no chunks of pepper or tomatoes. One of the main reasons for this is to avoid cheating. Say everybody else was doing the standard formula and you had tomato chunks in yours, and perhaps, you had a buddy at the judging table that knew to look for your tomato chunks. This is the same reason we don't do beans. Well, that and we believe the old-time cowboy cooks—the chuckwagon cooks—would want the cowboys to think they were getting more food, so they would dip beans out from one bowl and chili from another. We don't believe the old San Antonio chili queens used beans in theirs either. If you're at home and want to extend your chili for guests, go ahead and add beans. It's just a little more protein. But we don't use beans in competition chili."

In addition to individuals competing to cook, teams can compete in the show category. The show competition involves dressing up in crazy costumes, acting out entertaining shenanigans, and in general, displaying complete silliness for two hours. "Show teams have to qualify with the same point systems [as chili cooks] to compete in show at Terlingua," Roger says. "There are three categories of show teams: large (six or more members), small (up to six members) and now, there is a category for a one-person show."

The year Roger won in CASI, 2004, he also was a member of the first place large show team. "They award show right before they award chili, so I was already backstage with the show team," Roger says. "Then, they called my number for winning chili too. The guys didn't believe me, but I showed them my number and walked back out to claim the win."

To get an event sanctioned through CASI, the organizer must advertise the event in *The Terlingua Trails*, the CASI newsletter, thirty days before the event. "Technically, the information has to be turned in forty-five days in advance because there's a fifteen day cut off for getting information printed," Roger adds. "The chili year ends September 30, and the new year starts October 1 to qualify for the following year. Ending in September gives the tally master (the person keeping up with points) enough time to get invitations out for Terlingua.

"There are about 300 acres at the CASI site. CASI has eleven board members elected by the Great Peppers," Roger shares. "If you look at some of the old, old pictures, you'll see the celebrities and notables in the entertainment world involved in judging. That original event was a great getaway, and since everyone had such a great time, they decided to do it year after year."

Roger shared an article he was asked to write about Carroll Shelby, one of the founding fathers of the original cook-off.

CARROLL SHELBY
by Roger Foltz

I was told to write an article about the legendary Carroll Shelby, but I never met the man, and all I knew about him was what was in the newspapers. Oh, I did know he lived in Highland Park at one time, because I dated a girl who lived down the street and pointed out his house to me. That was about the time the Shelby Mustang was making its debut.

So I started research; I asked my friends and former TICC Champions Bob and Doris Coats what their recollections of Mr. Shelby were. Doris provided me with many documents to review in my research, and both told me tales of the old days cooking chili with Mr. Shelby.

According to an article in *Texas Monthly* (sorry can't find a date of the article) "CASI was founded in 1951 by an indefinite number of middle-aged, middle-class chili lovers. They are publishers, newspaper editors, prosperous attorneys, columnists, local television personalities, and ranking public relations men." This date would mean that CASI is now sixty-one years old! Another source states CASI was formed in the late '40s.

Most all chili cooks have heard about the first cook-off in Terlingua and all the hoopla around it. All that hoopla had a purpose; it was to attract attention to the 200,000-acre Chiricahua Ranch owned by Carroll Shelby and Attorney David Witts and hopefully, find a buyer for the Ranch. The main sponsor of Wick Fowler at that first cook-off was the Chili Appreciation Society International. Fowler was later known as the chief chef for Chili Appreciation Society International. It was supposed to be a onetime event in 1967, but realizing what a great party it was, they decided to do it again the following year. By the time of the second world championship in 1968, Carroll Shelby was the social director of the Terlingua Country Club.

Shelby was a judge at the world championships from at least

1968 until 1972, according to records. There was not a list of judges for 1973 and 1974.

From all the old articles written about chili and original *Chili Monthly Magazines*, Shelby got involved in chili cook-offs to raise money for charities. His desire for this was prompted when he suffered heart problems and became aware of so many people that needed assistance.

Richard Knight wrote in last month's *Trails* about the ambulance Shelby helped purchase for the Terlingua Medics. From Bob Coats, I learned that the vehicle was sent to Florida for a special paint job, costing much more than it would have cost locally here in Texas. Dodge Truck division, Stroh Brewing, and PepsiCo were among the sponsors who put up the $60,000 to buy and outfit the ambulance. Several other sponsors backed out after a ruckus over the cook-off, and Shelby made up the deficit by acquiring Chili's restaurants as a sponsor and including his own Original Texas Chili preparation mix as sponsors. There was a thank you letter to Shelby and the other sponsors signed by most, if not all, residents of Terlingua at the time.

In the 1980s, Shelby had moved from Ford to Dodge and became a benefactor of the Bottom of the Barrel Gang—Bob and Doris Coats, Richard and Carol Knight, Ken and Dusty Hudspeth, Steve and Jan Frisch, Barbra and Monty Britton, Paul Brian, Paul and Sylvia Wiseman, Doug Beigh, Bob and June Leclerc, Ken and Peggy Robbins, Jim Kitterman, and Dr. John and Nita Winters—and got them a Dodge van for team members use to and from cook-offs. If you check on these team members, you'll find four TICC champions!

From all I've read and heard about Carroll Shelby, he didn't cook competitive chili but was always there to help and support all cooks. He realized his fame would bring attention to the cook-offs and help the charities, but he seemed to be happy in the background, not always trying to be the one in the photos, just pleased to lend his name, stature, and resources when needed to a worthy cause.

Carroll Shelby's approach to chili: "The beauty of chili to me is that it's really a state of mind. It's just what you make it.

You can put anything in there you want, make it hot or mild, any blend of spices you feel like at the time. You make it up to suit your mood."

Carroll Shelby played a large part in the beginnings of competition chili cooking and the Chili Appreciation Society International.

And in the words of Billy the Kid, "Anyone who likes chili can't be all bad.

DEANNA CASTILLO

I went to visit with Deanna Castillo of the High Sierra Bar in Terlingua in the summer of 2015. We sat down to taste her award-winning recipe, and she showed me all her trophies she keeps at her office. "The cook-off put Terlingua on the map," says Deanna.

A woman of distinction in the chili community, Deanna credits learning the art of chili making from two championship cooks: Roger Foltz and Tom Dozier. Having placed well at multiple chili competitions, she hosts her own chili cook-off in January each year as a fundraising event for Ghost Town Charities. "Kathleen Tolbert Ryan's dad (Frank X. Tolbert) helped found the original international chili cook-off behind the store," Deanna shares. "She's a good friend of Herman and me." Herman Everett is Deanna's husband. He's visiting on his porch with the guys while Deanna and I take pictures. Her chili is to die for. "I start with two pounds of meat and roll it into little balls, like big meatballs. I'll get maybe eight big huge meatballs. Then once you cook the meat, add your liquids. Competition chili, it has to look the same: it's how you grind up your spices that make the flavors change. Mine is a basic recipe. You can add and take away.

"I got that recipe from two championship cooks that are really good friends that come in here all the time: Tom and Roger. Roger Foltz won in 2004. He's the one that helped me come up with that recipe. The first time, I cooked in Rankin, Texas, in 2012. It was a regional cook-off, and I won first place, the first time. The prize was a highly sought after bronze horny toad. After that, I started cooking and placing in the top ten lots of times. When I qualified to cook at the international cook-off in Terlingua in 2013, I got fourth place, which meant I automatically qualified to cook in 2014."

Deanna works her recipe based on the turn-in time. "If I'm cooking chili today to be judged at 5 p.m., I know I have a lot of beer drinkers, so I'm going to put in a lot of salt. If the judging takes place earlier in the day, Deanna decreases the amount of heat and salt. "If the judging is at noon, I pull my heat and my salt [back] a little," she says "because you're going to have judges judging it that don't want a lot of heat early in the day.

"In 2014, Kathleen [Tolbert Ryan] asked me if I would sponsor the rock, which is the trophy. I said, 'Sure, I'll sponsor the rock.'" Deanna also gives the Tolbert's Behind the Store competition other sponsorship money from High Sierra and El Dorado Hotel. "As rock sponsors, it was our turn during the fourth place announcements to step-up and announce the winners. When he [the announcer] gave Herman the ticket to make the announcement, it was as big of a surprise to me as it was to everyone else that I won the fourth place rock. Everyone laughed. After I had accepted the rock, I told Kathleen, 'Next year can I sponsor [the] first place rock?' She

said, 'Yes, of course.' I came in fourth both years, though."
Deanna has also cooked at the CASI site, but she hasn't
placed there as she has in the Behind the Store competition.
"Tolbert's Behind the Store is close knit," Deanna shares.
"CASI is big and huge with a lot of sponsors, a lot of events,
it's a lot of fun. Behind the Store is smaller. Besides, you need
twelve points to qualify for CASI. I live in Terlingua. You know
how hard it is to get twelve points?" She smiles and helps me
with my dishes. "It's a big production [making competition
chili]," she shares. "You have your table, chili pots, propane,
you have to cook outside, cutting boards...it's a big ordeal."

Herman walks in to check on us, and she asks him for his
famous black-eyed pea recipe. "I can't remember; I'm always drinkin'," Herman jokes. "We always have a big New
Year's Eve party, and he's always late to it," Deanna says. "He
always has to cook it in twenty minutes. Last year, he got
second place with it."

"I just cook the peas," says Herman, "with a pound of crispy
bacon, that's the secret. And I add green chiles that are
seeded. I submerge the peas in water with their snaps for
about forty-five minutes before I start cooking them, and
that's it."

When Deanna won the regional chili cook-off in Rankin, she
beat out 117 cooks for first place. "Another chili cook I met
along the chili trail was Tom Dozier," she says. "Tom won
CASI in 2010. In 2011, he got second place. He has a lot of titles and is sponsored by a lot of food companies. He helped
me tweak my recipe to what I now serve here at the restaurant." She says the restaurant recipe has given her a first
place win and a couple of fourth place finishes.

"Herman always helps me cook too. When Herman and I first
started dating in 2000 in Del Rio, he had his property here
and was building the hotel," says Deanna. "He always said he
was going to end up retiring in Terlingua, but I had two kids
from a previous marriage that I had to raise there in Del Rio,
so we built the hotel slowly. The restaurant opened in 2007,
and the hotel opened in 2001.

"I had a full-time job as a finance manager for a car dealership. In 2010, I became more ingrained in the Terlingua community. When my youngest graduated from high school and went to college, Herman said, 'It's time for you to quit your job and come to Terlingua.' I told him, 'I have to have a job. I have to do something.' So he said I could overlook the restaurant and hotel. I don't manage it really, though; I just overlook it—I have a great manager.

"I got into chili cooking because I have a lot of guests that come and stay for the cook-off. That's when Roger Foltz got me involved. He was a friend of High Sierra's who would always come and have beers.

"I have my own chili cook-off," Deanna says, "the last Saturday in January. It's all held on the grounds of the High Sierra. We have a Dutch oven cook-off at the same time, and it's grown to be such a popular event. I have over one hundred cooks come in. The community gets together, and they get to judge. Once it gets to the finals, we handpick our judges. We try to get a cook from each of the local restaurants to judge. The community is great. They come together and support my effort. All the money I raise at the chili cook-off goes back to my 501(c)(3), and we buy things like propane, medical, etc. The entry fees are twenty dollars to cook.

Cooking chili is my charity. I have a fund, and I help a lot of people." Deanna says the U.S. Open Chili Championship has chosen High Sierra as the site of their 2016 competition. Former locations of the event include Florida and California, but because of the success of Deanna's cook-off at High Sierra, the group chose to come to Terlingua in 2016.

KRIS HUDSPETH

Kris Hudspeth provides another perspective on the cook-off. He's been involved his entire lifetime and has served as public relations director for CASI. Originally from Irving, Texas, and now living in Garland, Texas, Kris was only six months old the first time his parents took him to the Terlingua chili cook-off. "The first time I went to Terlingua, Mom had won the world championship in ICS in 1984," Kris shares. "When Mom won ICS, she handed me to Carroll Shelby, and I sat on his lap while she went to collect her prize."

Kris's maternal grandmother, Doris, and her husband, Bob Coats, inspired Kris's mom to join them on the chili trail. "Doris got Mom hooked on cooking chili and going to Terlingua," shares Kris. "Then Dad started participating and served on the board in the late '80s. Doris and Bob are the only husband and wife team to have won. Doris won in 1991, and Bob won in 1999.

"The first time I went to cook, I was nineteen years old. I was just out of high school. Bob and Doris told me the first time I qualified I could come stay with them, and they would pay for everything. In high school, I played football and baseball. I have a sister that's four years younger, so there was a period of time when Doris and Mom quit cooking because we were on the go all the time. I played one hundred baseball games a year between spring football and fall football. We didn't have time to cook competitively then.

"But Doris ran a cook-off at Lake Lewisville. It was a Texas Open and because it was a state championship, it automatically qualifies the top three cooks, unless there are 150 or more in which case it qualifies the top five. I came in second which meant I was qualified to cook at Terlingua. When they called my number, my smile got bigger. Doris said 'Oh shit! I guess he's going to Terlingua this year, Bob.'"

Kris recalls that because he was underage, Bob and Doris would only allow him to drive them around. "They wouldn't let me out of their sight," he says. "I wasn't old enough to drink legally. If I wanted to have a beer, I had to do it very discreetly, right by them. I had a six pack that lasted me the whole weekend. That year I came in twelfth in Terlingua.

"I didn't start cooking again until almost ten years later in 2011," Kris remembers. "I was going to college, majoring in beer. It [Terlingua] just wasn't that big of a deal to me during that time. Finally in 2011, Mom and I looked at each other and decided we weren't going to get to do this with Bob and Doris much longer. They were getting older, and we decided we didn't know how much longer they would be cooking. So 2011 was my first time back as an adult to Terlingua, and I haven't missed a year since.

"As a director, I have to be down there for a week. But my mentality is that I want to compete. I don't want just to watch other people cook while we are in Terlingua. I do everything I can to get qualified and, the good Lord willing, every year I've been qualified.

"The people that go down there that are regular chili cooks that don't get qualified—it's no big deal. But I'm a big competitor, and it makes me sick to my stomach to think I couldn't qualify. I cooked forty times one year, and I didn't get my first point until August 14-15. I ran up fifteen points in twenty-five days to get qualified. Our recipe finally got hot, but I had to be smart about where I went and cooked. My drinking and chili-cooking buddy and I sat down with the *Terlingua Trails* and looked at where cook-offs were and what was coming up. We decided to hit Lake Tawakoni—four times.

"Up until the end right before Terlingua, I still needed two points. There is a cook-off the weekend before the state fair opens. I thought I'd just get qualified there. But there were eighty-five of the best cooks in North Texas with former world championships there. So we decided our best chance at getting qualification points was to cook in Paris, [Texas]. They were about to announce first place and my name hadn't been called." He told his mom that he would be mad if they'd driven all the way to Paris and he didn't win. But as luck would have it, Kris won the Paris cook-off and qualified for Terlingua.

Kris says he subscribes to the KISS theory when it comes to his chili recipe. "I keep it simple, stupid," he says. "If it doesn't work, it's not my fault. Cooking chili is a lot like golf in that it's a most humbling sport. You can be a great athlete and completely suck at golf. Chili is the same way: you can have a great recipe that has won two world championships at Terlingua and use the same recipe and lose at another tournament. It's ninety percent luck and ten percent recipe. Every week, we have a different set of judges, and they all want something different. If you're behind a really great chili and your chili is good, you're going to score. If your chili is really hot, and the judge doesn't like it, you're not going to score—especially if you get to Terlingua. If you're lucky enough to get to the finals table, the judges have been working for four hours, and your chili is stone cold at that point. It has lost the majority of the spice bloom and everything. At that point you either have a good recipe and you're damn lucky, or you don't. It's a complete crap shoot. I have friends that will mix a new recipe if it's late in the year and they aren't qualified. I keep telling them to quit changing things. 'Just cook your recipe,' I tell them. 'Quit messin' with it. If you mess with it, you're going to screw things up.'

"This is the first year [2015] we made a wholesale change in our chili, meaning we changed chili powder flavors completely. There are the little idiosyncrasies we think about.

"I'm blessed that I have the grandparents that I do. Once Doris won in '91, her goal was to get Bob his world championship. Bob has what we call in our family 'the ultimate Oreo.' He was on a roll all year [during] 1999-2000. He was the hottest chili cook in the world and the luckiest S-O-B I've ever known. I got to go with him to the men's state cook-off in San Marcos. There were five hundred men-only cooks. In 1999, Bob won that cook-off against five hundred other chilies. He turns around and is tied for first with four people in Terlingua and won the tiebreaker. He turns around after that, and in September, wins the men's state cook-off again. He sandwiched his TICC championship with back-to-back men's state championship wins. We have over three hundred cooks in Terlingua, and he beat five hundred cooks two years in a row at men's state. His is called 'the ultimate Oreo' because no one has done that since then. Men's state is not near the spectacle it once was. To be able to win that many cook-offs with that many cooks is a once in a lifetime achievement."

Kris says that he, his mom, and grandparents Doris and Bob all cook the exact same recipe. "It was developed through a lot of hard work, tears, finger-pointing, and crying. No, I'm kidding. We were at Mom's house when we decided we were going to start cooking. Mom and Doris were working on a new recipe. We are blessed with Doris. For a smoker and beer drinker, she has one of the most refined palates of anyone I've ever met in my life. I'd put her palate in a blind taste test of anyone in the world. She can taste a chili and tell you immediately what is giving it a funky taste. They can take it over to Doris, and she'll say, 'Yep, it's this,' or 'Where do you buy this from? No, buy it from here, that will fix it.' They will buy it, cook it again and it will be better the next week." Kris says he can taste test chili and recommend adjustments too, but that his palate does not come close to the sensitivity that Doris has.

"One night when we were getting ready to develop a recipe, we set up four pots of chili on mom's stove," Kris says. They had a group of friends come over and test all the chili. That's how they arrived at a consensus as to which of the four pots of chili was the best. "These were just non-chili cooks that we knew—friends of mine from high school, friends of Mom's from work, my sister and brother-in-law—people that knew what competition chili was but didn't have skin in the game. And that's how we developed our recipe," he explains.

Kris has been involved with CASI his entire life. He was a CASI scholarship recipient (2002) and has served on the board of directors. "One reason I'm giving back to the organization through leadership is because my sister and I received scholarships. You won't meet a greater group of people; you won't have more fun; you won't drink any more in the world than you will hanging out with chili cooks." Kris says some of his best friends are chili cooks. He says they come from all different walks of life. "I have a buddy on the board with me that's a multi-millionaire dairy farmer. Others are COO's of Fortune 500 companies. There are some so broke they don't know what to do with themselves. I wanted to repay the organization for all the good times that I've had and the scholarship money. The influence the organization has made on my life has been great."

The CASI organization has an eleven-member board. "We are a one hundred percent volunteer organization," Kris explains. "Every year we elect four directors. Two of them get a three-year term, and two get a two-year term. Every other year, we elect an executive director. We also have a group of grass-roots local chapters called pods that run with a five-person mini-board of directors with one director elected from each of the different pods."

The Board is responsible for all aspects of hosting the Terlingua International Chili Competition: getting insurance, public relations requests, marketing, day-to-day business, scholarship funding, and maintenance, etc. "We do all the heavy lifting in the organization," Kris explains. "The pods and the everyday chili cooks are our bread and butter. That's where all the money for charity is raised. There are sixty-six pods worldwide. To be a seated pod, you have to have twenty-five paid members, you have to have one pod cook-off, and you have to fill out an annual pod report of what has taken place in your pod over the year. You have to send someone as a representative to our Great Peppers meeting. All of our board meetings are open to the public, but there is one meeting a year where we require all of our Great Peppers to be at the meeting or to send a delegate. The Great Peppers meeting is a tacky state of the union we hold in September. It's where we give all of our end of the year financial reports and make any rule changes. The Great Peppers vote, and the board implements."

Kris says the way to become a Great Pepper is to join as a member of a pod and get involved in the pod. "When pod elections come up, you put your name in the hat. You'll want to show up to your pod meetings. Otherwise, you'll get stuck with a job you don't want," says Kris.

SCOTT AND JENNY TURNER

Born in San Angelo, Scott moved all over West Texas while his father worked as a law enforcement officer, then later as a drilling fluids engineer.

"The oil bust in 1981 brought our family to Big Bend," Scott shares. He says his dad had trouble finding a job in the oil field and had some buddies that "ran around" Terlingua and told him it was "an up and coming place"—a great place to live. "I found myself in the La Kiva parking lot in a 14-foot RV trailer with Mom and Dad, [my] sister, two parrots, two cats, and Dudley, the 95-pound Saint Bernard/Doberman pinscher mix. I woke up the first morning, walked across Terlingua Creek and thought I was in Mexico. But I was just wandering around Benji Bell's property. Dad was hired as the foreman at Three Bar Ranch outside Terlingua, and we lived there all through my high school years."

Jenny was born in Maryland and grew up in the Upper Peninsula of Michigan. "I moved to Colorado and became a river guide in the late '80s before I moved to Texas," Jenny shares. "In the early '90s, I heard a rumor about a river that was running (and companies that were hiring) in the Big Bend of Texas. I was skeptical, but I loaded up my black lab and drove my white International Scout to the border. I was stunned at what I found there. I had visited Austin but had no idea Texas had such magnificent mountains and a river! I came to work one spring break season and never left. I met my husband during that fateful spring break season. By June, I was hooked: on the southwest Texas desert and the tall, handsome cowboy that sure could two-step!"

Together, they now own Mountain Trails Lodge in Fort Davis and Come & Take It BBQ in Alpine. "I've been coming to the Terlingua cook-off since 1993," Jenny shares. My husband's family worked the Terlingua chili cook-off Behind the Store when Carolina & Arturo owned the store. On my first visit to the cook-off behind the store, I ended up helping them serve beer under the pavilion."

Scott has been coming to the Terlingua cook-off since 1981. "I was about thirteen or fourteen years old the first time

I went to the cook-off. I drove an old, broken-down, blue Datsun full of mesquite roots I'd gathered between Three Bar Ranch and the campsite. It always seemed to be frigid cold and sleeting. Gabriel and I would drive around and sell bundles of firewood to people who were freezing. I did that every year until I joined the army." Girls were a big reason he went to the cook-off too. "When you're a young single guy in Terlingua, there aren't a lot of options. We were going to go where the people were," Scott laughs.

"South Brewster County defies a single description," Scott says. "Native Americans and Hispanics blend with descendants of early Anglo settlers, shopkeepers, and ranchers, like the Fulchers. In the late '60s and '70s, the region attracted a counter-culture population of artists, hippies, musicians, curanderas, and people generally hoping to escape civilization. The creation of Big Bend National Park, better roads making the region more accessible, and the advent of river companies running the Rio Grande brought more tourists to the region resulting in growth in the service industry. More recently, with the introduction of more reliable electricity and high-speed Internet, the area has seen an insurgence of city dwellers who are now able to work from their homes in paradise, alongside those who are trying their hand at 'off-grid' living."

MICHAEL TIERNEY

"I was two years old when the cook-off started in '67, then Dad (Tom Tierney) broke away when I was twelve or so," shares Michael Tierney. "My dad was the self-proclaimed judge of Terlingua.

"The way I remember the story is that one of the guys had 200,000 acres in Terlingua and was trying to get rid of it. Dad was doing PR for Ford and worked for Carroll Shelby, who had also bought land down in Terlingua. Dad suggested they have a chili cook-off. He was friends with Frank [Tolbert] from the *Dallas Morning News*. Being a writer, Frank was all over the concept. They brought in H.A. Smith from California, who said he made the best chili, and that's how it got started. It was a PR move done on a joke.

"They weren't college guys; just businessmen that wanted to have a good drunken weekend." Michael says. "It was a funny thing that started with six or eight guys that just wanted to have a good time. They had such a fun time; they decided to go back again. It's like a good hunting trip with guys that just want to go back every year.

"I've been to Terlingua numerous times," shares Michael. "I've gone to the Rio Grande and Lajitas. They had twenty-five cent tacos and twenty-five cent tequila shots and a pool table across the border. There was a barge with a rope, and they'd pull you across. I've been to the area, but I've never actually attended the cook-off."

The way Michael recalls it, the Terlingua Racing Team was developed during the early years too. "Shelby was with Ford, Neale was a designer for Ford, Dad was doing PR for Ford, so they decided to make a racing team," says Michael. "Bill Neale scribbled the Terlingua Racing Team logo on a napkin. They needed a logo and decided to go with a jackrabbit because it was a little more Podunk. It was done on a lark too. I know at one point there was a monkey involved around 1977 or 1978, but I can't remember the story."

Michael says that his dad believed that anything could be done with a group of people as long as no one person took credit for all of it. He says he took that to mean that as long as people are willing to work together, then anything can be accomplished.

Michael says his dad never entered the cook-off but judged it once or twice in its beginning years. He says his dad says of the experience, "You destroy what you create." Tom felt that the advent of the cook-off changed the town from a "nothing" town to one that became more well known.

Michael uses Wick Fowler's 2-Alarm Chili Kit with extra onions when he cooks chili at home. "One thing my dad always taught me: no beans in chili." Michael says that when he would visit his dad in Dallas, they would always go to Shanghai Jimmy's and order the chili rice. "It had a layer of rice, a layer of chili, more rice, more chili, cheddar cheese, on-ions, and sweet pickle relish on top," he describes.

DEBBIE WEBB

"I go to Big Bend because it's God's country," shares Michael Tierney's sister Debbie. "The first time I went with my dad, mom, and one of my sisters, and a family friend of my dad's. We went rafting down the Rio Grande through Santa Elena Canyon in one day. When we were coming out of the canyon, it was almost night." She says the wind was so strong that each time they took a stroke with their paddles, the wind would push them backward. "My dad and the guide got in the water to pull us through it," she concludes.

Michael suggested I call his sisters for backup stories, and I got to visit with Debbie on the phone about her memory from her dad Tom Tierney's involvement with the Ter-lingua chili cook-off. "It was men only in the beginning," Debbie says. "It's like a diamond; everyone has a different perspective on this thing."

"My understanding is the guys were all playing poker one night," Debbie shares. "One turned to Dad and said, 'If you're such a great PR guy, what can you do with this ghost town?' Dad got with Frank X. Tolbert and started this dialogue with this guy up North about who has the best chili.

"During that first event, they were all sleeping on sleeping bags," Debbie says. The next morning her dad got out of his bag, and a tarantula crawled out after him. "During the second year, they actually hired banditos, if you will, who came and stole the ballot box for the chili contest and went across the river to make the second year a 'draw.' So it was still all just for fun."

Debbie attended the cook-off in October of 1978. "They had an airstrip," she remembers. "People were flying in their private planes, and it had grown a lot by then. It was pretty amazing. They had designated official judges. It was something you could only do in the '70s. People came from far and wide, in motorcycles and RV's. By then it had gone global. It was becoming so well known. It was still kind of a

guy's thing, but girls were there by now. It's not for the faint of heart environmentally. It's hot.

"Carroll Shelby took his group out of it and back to California. But Terlingua was the launching pad for all chili cook-offs. Those who continued the cook-off tradition in Terlinuga created a system whereby cook-off participants had to earn a certain amount of points from other cook-offs throughout the year in order to qualify for and be invited to cook at the grand finale in Terlingua.

"My dad and Frank [Tolbert] and Dave [Witts]—they had all those posters on their walls. These were all guys in their mid-forties having a good time in life in Texas, each respecting each other's talents and abilities. Frank, Shelby, Dad, Witts—they were all just good, hardworking guys doing what they did best. They were fun-loving guys. Frank really picked up the baton and got it in the national newspapers that the challenge had started, which created a whole reading frenzy between the two competitors. Back then, there was no Internet, so by design, this is how the dialogue happened. The chili cook-off is a manifestation of what you can create when you're having fun."

Debbie used to do the website for Marfa tourism. "Now people come out there for everything, but back then it was just Marfa," she smiles and shares. "I worked for the Texas Travel Industry Association and Texas tourism at all levels. The board used to go out there for the board meetings at Terlingua too. We went across the river for food. It was made up of an extraordinary group of men. The Texas Travel Industry Association work is something most people don't think about, but it opened the door to the entire state for me. People in tourism enjoy what they do and are passionate about their cities. I think we forget to pass forward that passion trumps money sometimes.

"Like my brother, we are diehards with the Wick Fowler

2-Alarm or False-Alarm, and after that, we put it on rice with cheese, crackers, and celery.

Going into the fall, it's hearty comfort food on a Friday night with crushed up saltines, onions, and cheese. We've been making it that way for years. That, for us, works."
Debbie was pregnant with her firstborn when she went to Terlingua with her dad. "My dad was so excited to have me go and be there," she remembers. "He knew everybody. At that point, they had been doing it for years. It was infectious. When you're seeing your dad like a little kid having a ball with the guys and not in a standard work environment, that was special. Back then, we didn't see our dads in that light. We saw him in khakis and boots and going off to work. So what was so infectious about the cook-off to me was his joy."

DIEGO PALACIOS AND BILL IVEY

In July of 2015, Diego Palacios and Bill Ivey sat down with me to discuss the pulse of the Terlingua cook-off. It was so hot out that the ice in our tea melted in minutes. The temperature registered over a hundred on the porch, so we circled around a table inside the Starlight to enjoy a bowl of red and saltines.

"When I first started doing chili cook-offs, everyone camped out in the ghost town," Bill recalls. "It's interesting because a lot of those same people I saw sleeping in the back of a pickup or station wagon in the '70s are pulling up in a $250,000 motorhome [now]," he smiles as I drip a big chunk of chili all over my notebook. "They're not into sleeping on the ground anymore.

"It's a lot more organized now than in the old days. They have a staunch set of rules they go by. Some like it; some don't. There are two now. The smaller one is more of a reunion for the folks that have been coming forever, where the CASI site is a very serious contest. To win is an incredibly high-esteemed honor.

"A lot of locals leave during that week, but not because of the chili cook-off," Bill explains, rolling up a sleeve, "mostly because of the law enforcement. If you have a dirty license plate, they will pull you over. I was coming down to give a talk to the school kids about Day of the Dead and got pulled over for going ten percent over the speed limit."

Diego chimes in saying that you'll see six police officers between the two sites—one for each mile between the sites. "Employees come late because they got pulled over twice in one day," he says.

"At the CASI site, they don't allow you to use fresh ingredients," Diego explains. "They make you use dry ingredients and the same cut of beef (80/20 ground beef). Basically, they have 150 of the same kinds of chili. It's very regulated judging. So it's kind of the best of the same. It's become a party for the spectators, though. The people that go are serious about the food. They've been coming for years and they have their camps. They prepare not only chili but also brisket, ribs, margaritas, beans. It's a weeklong event now.

"At the CASI site, there are RVs stacked against each other with no hookups. Everyone is self-contained. A lot of the cooks that come in RVs have power generators, and a lot of folks just camp out."

CHILI HISTORY TIMELINE

As a reminder, the chili history and lore accounts for three main chili cooking groups: (1) The Frank X. Tolbert – Wick Fowler group (Tolbert's Behind the Store) (2) The Chili Appreciation Society International group (CASI), and (3) The International Chili Society group (ICS). When H. Allen Smith said the "chief ingredients of all chili are fiery envy, scalding jealousy, scorching contempt, and sizzling scorn," little did he know how true those words would ring for the great chili divide that would unfold.

From 1967 to 1974, it was one big chili family. But in 1975, the ICS group led by Carroll Shelby took their world championship to California, and the Texans kept theirs at Terlingua. In 1983, the Texan group would split. CASI held their cook-off at one site, while Tolbert's took their competition "behind the store". To date, the three groups host their own individual versions of the world championships: ICS in California and Tolbert's and CASI both in Terlingua. The latter two follow tradition and always occur on the first Saturday of November.

1966: *A Bowl of Red* by Frank X. Tolbert is originally published.

1967: This marks the first year of the world championship. The challenge is between Wick Fowler and H. Allen Smith. Of the three judges, Hallie Stilwell gives her vote to H. Allen, Floyd Schneider gives his to Wick, and Dave Witts spits out both, claiming burned taste buds. Thus, the first year is called a tie. The ingredient list for chili includes basil in 1967.

1968: The spirit of fun journalism continues the second year. Woodruff "Wino Woody" DeSilva, replaces H. Allen Smith and cooks his chili against Wick Fowler's. Scott Carpenter, an astronaut, serves as the head judge. After learning about cheating in the ballot box, Carpenter requests a re-vote. But before they could open the ballot box, a masked bandit waving a gun comes and steals the ballot box, throwing it down a mine. Therefore, the second year has no winner either, although the Tolbert-Fowler group gives "Wino Woody" DeSilva the victory. An unusual ingredient in DeSilva's pot is woodruff, an herb.

1969: H.Allen Smith publishes his book *The Great Chili Confrontation*. C.V. Wood, Jr. ("Woody"), an Amarillo native who built Disneyland for Walt Disney and brought the London Bridge to Lake Havasu, brings his best chili recipe all the way from Beverly Hills to the competition in Terlingua against Wick Fowler and Joe DeFrates. Woody takes the victory with some Hollywood actresses by his side, and the cook-off has its first winner. His winning recipe includes chicken and pork chops but no beef. It contains tomato sauce, broths, spices, onions, peppers, and a can of Budweiser.

1970: The new International Chili Society (ICS) forms and endorses the 1970 cook-off. "Chiligettes" fight for their right to cook with the men for the first time this year, and as such, Janice Constantine of Midland, Texas, cooks accompanied by a male violinist in a tuxedo. Wick Fowler claims the championship with his 2-Alarm chili recipe, with which he would go on to create a successful chili spice mix company. In his recipe, he offers variations to the 2-Alarm chili: for 1-Alarm chili—

use only half of the red pepper; for False-Alarm chili—leave out the red pepper; and for 3-Alarm chili or hotter—merely add hot pepper.

1971: Competitors come from Texas, New York, Illinois, California, and beyond. Woody wins his second world championship at the fifth annual Terlingua chili cook-off with the same recipe he used from 1969. The Tolbert-Fowler group claims that Woody won the "Super Bowl" and also credits George Wright with winning the world championship that year.

1972: Terlingua cook-off co-founder and 2-Alarm Chili creator Wick Fowler passes away from Lou Gehrig's disease. Thus, the 1972 world championship cook-off is dedicated to his honor. Future cook-offs will go on to donate several thousands of dollars to Lou Gehrig's causes. This year, Tolbert's book is updated, and cook-off co-founder Carroll Shelby announces that his Original Texas Brand Chili Mix is on the market, while Woody announces his retirement from cook-offs. Howard Winsor wins the championship with his recipe, which starts by combining onions, garlic, and water in a blender followed by chiles to create a chile pulp that he uses in making his bowl of red.

1973: After five years of cooking at the world's, Joe DeFrates of Illinois wins his first world championship with a very basic recipe using meat, tomato sauce, Chili Man Chili mix, and a dash of Tabasco.

1974: The first female world champion Allegani Jani Schofield wins with her Hot Pants Chili, which utilizes mole paste. The ICS group holds its world championship in Terlingua this year, but Shelby and Woody will be integral in moving the ICS group competitions to California. The remaining Texas group will eventually split in 1983 resulting in the creation of three world championships.

1975: The ICS World Championship Chili Cook off takes place at the Tropico Goldmine in Rosamond, California, and the Children's Hospital of Los Angeles will be the beneficiary. Joe DeFrates again takes the victory with his simple Chili

Man Chili recipe that includes only three main ingredients. Back in Terlingua, Susie Watson adds a feather to her cap winning the world championship in Texas. Woodruff "Wino Woody" DeSilva and H. Allen Smith pass away joining Wick Fowler to compete in the chili cook-off in the sky.

1976: In Terlingua, Albert S. Agnor takes the crown using his mother's recipe which *Southern Living* had previously published. The U.S. Navy veteran wins several more times before developing his signature chili mix and opening his restaurant, both named The Chili House (www.agnorchilimix.com). His championship chili inspires the Texas legislature to name chili the state dish of Texas (H.C.R. No. 18).

Back in California, Shelby and Woody hire Jim West as the first executive director of the ICS. Rudy Valdez, a full-blooded Ute Indian, wins the ICS cook-off which includes three prizes: a year's lease on a Datsun pickup, a pair of Larry Mahan boots, and a Rival crockpot. His winning recipe includes celery among other more traditional chili ingredients.

Hondo Crouch makes his way to chili heaven this year.

1977: The ICS group reports over 20,000 in attendance at the California world championship. Jay Pennington takes the win with a standard recipe that also includes the use of bell peppers. Tom Griffin takes the win in Terlingua with his famous Buzzard's Breath Chili.

1978: At the ICS competition, the American Spice Trade Association creates a new award for the cook using the most spices in their recipe. Max Vallejo of Oregon wins this specialty award while Laverne Harris wins a check for $15,000 and the world championship title. Laverne's traditional recipe calls for the use of Budweiser. Richard Simon takes the win in Terlingua.

1979: Wayland Walker walks away victorious at the Terlingua site while Joe and Shirley Stewart win ICS with their Reno Red recipe.

1980 Bob Moore wins the Terlingua cook-off. *Chili-Lovers' Cookbook* by Al Fischer and Mildred Fischer prints his recipe, which calls for a can of Lone Star beer. At ICS, Bill Pfeiffer takes the win with his Capital Punishment recipe.

1981: Bill Douglas (who later drives a tour bus for Miley Cyrus) wins in Terlingua. In California, ICS holds their event at the Hollywood Park race track with over sixty contenders. Fred and Linda Drexel take home the win with their Butterfield Stage Line Chili, which utilizes beef brisket and lean ground pork, Budweiser beer, and other traditional ingredients.

1982: Tom Skipper wins the Terlingua cook-off. Over in California, ICS moves from Hollywood Park to Universal Studios where Bill Pfeiffer takes a second world championship win with his Los Venganza Del Almo recipe raising his total championship earnings to $40,000.

1983: The ICS moves back to the Tropico Goldmine where Harold Timber beats out seventy-four contestants from around the world. But over in Texas, another rumble in the chili family percolates and a split occurs over disagreements in how to run the cook-off. The two Texas groups (Tolbert's and CASI) continue to hold their version of their world championships in Terlingua simultaneously on the first Saturday of November. Paul Brian takes the win at the CASI site. His recipe suggests stirring in more chili powder as needed to tighten the stew to desired consistency. Dave Talbot wins over at Tolbert's.

1984: Former Texas State Champion Dusty Hudspeth buys her family a new house with the $25,000 she won with her Bottom Of The Barrel Gang Ram Tough Chili recipe at the ICS World Championship. Steve Weaver wins at the CASI site in Terlingua, and John Billy Murray wins at the Tolbert site.

1985: Wes Richey wins at the CASI site in Terlingua, and Jim Ivy won at Tolbert's. At ICS, Carol and Dave Hancock win with their Shotgun Willie Chili named after their friend Willie Nelson.

1986: The chili world championships mark their twentieth consecutive year. Dorene Ritchey wins at the Tolbert site in Terlingua with her 5-R Chili, and Bobby Aldridge wins at the

CASI site. ICS starts a tradition singing "God Bless America" to kick-off the cook-off that year, and Jim Beaty wins with his Sespe Creek Chili recipe.

1987: Margo Knudson becomes the fifth woman to win the world championships in ICS, while over in Terlingua, Steve Strattman wins at Tolbert's, and David Henson wins at CASI.

1988: Pepto Bismol joins as an ICS sponsor. Alongside the Tulsa Jaycees, the sponsors develop the Titanic Bowl of Red, then drove the 1,000-gallon chili pot from Tulsa to California and sold chili for charity for ICS that year. Hope and Monty Spuregon tie the chili knot on national television as they say their vows on the main stage at ICS. Linda and Kenton Stafford win at ICS with their 7/8's Chili recipe. Maxine Reed wins at Tolbert's in Terlingua, and Lynn Hejtmancik wins over at the CASI site.

1989: Phil Walter, also known as "Tarantula Jack" wins the ICS with Tarantula Jack's Thundering Herd Buffalo Tail Chili recipe just a few days before a nearby space shuttle landing at Edwards Air Force base. Johnny Lee performs, and the list of celebrity attendees continues to swell at the ICS site. Dawn Dish Soap is a sponsor and conducts a world championship dish washing competition in which Sheila Sowell of Abilene, Texas, wins a dream kitchen valued at $15,000. Meanwhile in Texas, Ruthann Newman wins at the Tolbert's site in Terlingua, and Barbara Britton wins at CASI.

1990: In Terlingua, Jerry Hunt wins at CASI and Jerry Thomas wins at Tolbert's. David Valega wins at ICS with his Backdoor Chili recipe.

1991: ICS holds its last competition at the Tropico Goldmine, and Randy Robinson wins with his Road Meat Chili recipe. And in Terlingua, Dorene Ritchey wins at Tolbert's, and Doris Coats wins at CASI.

1992: Dorene Ritchey wins again at Tolbert's in Terlingua while Cindy (Reed) Wilkins takes the win at CASI. At ICS, Dr. Ed Pierczynski wins at ICS with his recipe called Doc's Secret Remedy, which calls for London broil and sausage.

1993: Cindy (Reed) Wilkins wins a second consecutive year at CASI, and Bill Coad wins over at Tolbert's. Cathy Wilkey's Puppy's Breath Chili wins at ICS, which moved over to Reno, Nevada, and grew into a two-day festival. (Side note, Cindy has a heart attack between her two wins.)

1994: *Good Morning America* airs the start of their show from the main stage at ICS in Reno, where Bill and Karen Ray win with their Mountain Express Chili. In Texas, Dani Ritchey wins at Tolbert's, and Jim Hendrick wins at CASI.

1995: Brian Peddigrew wins at Tolbert's in Terlingua while Colleen Wallace wins at CASI. ICS grows into a three-day event when Norm and Bobbi Gaul beat more than two hundred competitors with their A-H Reamer Chili Company recipe.

1996: Bo Prewitt wins at CASI in Terlingua, and Bob Plager wins Tolbert's with his Pools Brew Chili. Georgia Weller's Southern Chili Georgia-Style recipe wins her the world championship title over at ICS.

1997: Glenn Dickey takes the victory at CASI and Dorene Ritchey wins a fourth time at Tolbert's. Steve Falkowski wins ICS with his Gold Miner's Chili.

1998: Kathy LeGear wins at ICS with her 24 Karat Chili recipe, while Carol West wins at CASI, and Bob Plager wins at Tolbert's again.

1999: Maud Swick wins the ICS championship with her Zanjero Red Chili while James Barker wins at Tolbert's, and Bob Coats—reveling in a major winning streak on the chili trail—wins at CASI.

2000: Bonnie Mosley wins at Tolbert's, Dixie Johnson wins at CASI, and Jim Weller, who started cooking in 1983, wins at ICS with his Macktown Chili recipe.

2001: Randy Moore wins at CASI, and Alan Greiner wins at Tolbert's while George Swick wins ICS with his Swick and Swick Chili.

2002: Clif Dugan wins at Tolbert's, Pat Pilchiek wins at CASI, and retired L.A. County Deputy Sheriff Ron Burt wins ICS with his Warning Shot Chili – Runs for Your Life.

2003: Wilderness guide Bob Wetzel of Montana wins ICS with his Bronco Bob's Chili, Ted Hume III wins at Tolbert's, and Honey Jones takes the glory at CASI.

2004: Roger Foltz wins at CASI, his first time cooking at the CASI championship. Linda Odom wins at Tolbert's by one point over Roger Foltz, and Kathleen Hipskind wins ICS with her Dago Reds Wop 'n Good Chili.

2005: Tom Burrows wins at Tolbert's, Margaret Nadeau wins at CASI and Doug Wilkey wins ICS with his Dog Breath Chili, which mixes breakfast sausage with coarse ground tri-tip beef.

2006: J.R. Knudson's Rough and Ready Chili wins at ICS, Bob Plager wins again at Tolbert's, and Dana Plocheck wins at CASI. Dana is the first to win CASI using ground meat instead of cut meat.

2007: Jerry Buma wins ICS with Booma's Revenge, Mike "BB" Hughes at Tolbert's, and first-timer Debbie Ashman wins at CASI.

2008: Susan Dean wins at CASI, Billy Bob Weatherly wins at Tolbert's, and Georgia Weller returns to ICS and wins again (she also won in 1996) with her Southern Chili recipe.

2009: Maureen Barrett's Almost Famous Red Chili wins at ICS; Margaret Nadeau wins at CASI again (she also won in 2005), and Jim Stoddard wins at Tolbert's.

2010: Christine Knight wins at Tolbert's, Tom Dozier wins at CASI, and Thomas J. Hoover, Jr. wins at ICS with his 2010 Happy Trails! Chili.

2011: John Jepson wins ICS with a recipe that calls for Rancho de Chimayo Hot New Mexico Chile Powder while George Odom wins at Tolbert's, and Larry Walton wins at CASI—his first time to cook at a CASI championship.

2012: Bob Plager, who has been cooking competitive chili since 1980 and has cooked in all three competitions winning Tolbert's several times, wins ICS. His Pools Brew Chili recipe calls for pitted prunes and other more traditional ingredients. Ted Hume III wins at Tolbert's for the second time, and T.J. Cannon wins at CASI.

2013: David Lazarus begins a winning streak at Tolbert's, Brian Spencer wins at CASI, and Bob Plager returns to ICS for another win.

2014: David Lazarus wins the second time at Tolbert's, and Jason Goins wins at CASI. After cooking chili for twenty years all across the country with his wife, Mike Stevens wins ICS with his Yakety Yak Ranch Chili.

2015: David Lazarus comes back to Tolbert's for a third consecutive win, James Burns wins at CASI, and David Hipskind wins at ICS.

CHILI COOKING TIPS FROM THE EXPERTS

If you're new to making chili, some of the chili recipes might read strangely. For example, you'll read instructions that call for adding "Spice Dump #1" and "Spice Dump #2." These "dumps" are referring to a homemade blend of spices the cook puts together to form a mixture to be added into the chili during different stages of the cooking process. Some recipes call for as many as four dumps strategically spread out over time to enhance flavor.

You'll read about "floating a pepper," which is an instruction to the cook to let a pepper (typically a jalapeño) stew on top of the chili while it's cooking which results in softening the pepper so that its juices seep out into the chili. Some recipes will call for you to further incorporate the pepper by carefully squeezing its juice into the pot of cooking chili.

Many chili cooks suggest refrigerating the chili overnight to let the spices intensify and create a new flavor profile. Competition chili cooks don't have the luxury of time to let their chili rest. As such, they have developed cooking techniques that give big flavor to just one spoonful. This is important since a judge must taste several chilies during any given competition. Some bites will still be hot in temperature upon tasting, but the latter chilies will often have cooled to room temperature or colder if it is windy outside. Because competition cooks are challenged to prepare a taste of chili that will pack a punch no matter when the judges taste the sample, competition chili tends to condense more flavor into one bite because it's that one bite that decides the competitors placement in the cook-off. Home cooks can relax a little more with the spices.

New cooks might tinker with other ingredients such as chocolate, peanut butter, beer, tomato jam, jalapeño jelly, or onion jam, all ingredients that go surprisingly well in chili, although I don't recommend using them all together. Plenty of opinions and rituals in the chili world exist as to how to make the best pot. Below is more advice from the chili pros:

Deanna Castillo
Competition chili cook Deanna Castillo recommends, "Give yourself at least two hours to cook a bowl of chili." She says simmering it for a few hours draws out the flavor. She also recommends pre-mixing your spices together before adding them to your chili when competing. During the competition, she tosses her spice mix into a coffee bean grinder right before she adds them to her chili. As for her favorite pot to use for cooking? "I always use a stainless steel chili pot that has a heavy bottom."

Roger Foltz
Award winning chili cook Roger Foltz says that the key to back heat—the heat that rises to your palate after the first initial taste—is white pepper. "If you get a chili that is too hot people say to use raw potato, but I think it takes all the other spices out, too. So put a DROP with an eye dropper of vodka in; alcohol will take out some of the heat. Be careful when you doctor your chili; lots of chili is ruined in the last fifteen minutes by people screwing with it." Roger says to trust your recipe and to "write down any changes you make if you need to change something.

"Chili cooks are very generous in helping new people," Roger says. "We've got to survive. Doris Coats says: 'You can cook my recipe; you *cannot* cook my chili.' We will give you the quantities of powders, but we will do something a little different each time."

Roger says that all the recipes address salt or heat. "If the judges have been drinking for two hours, add extra heat and salt to your chili. If I'm running a judging table, I like to have an equal amount of men and women judges, because each one's taste buds are going to be different." He says that this gives each chili a better chance. "More guys will want all salt, where women's taste buds are a little more delicate in tasting flavors. Doris Coats is incredible at tasting and telling what the chili needs—one-quarter ounce this or that. She's a great help in adjusting recipes."

Kris Hudspeth

Third generation competition chili cook Kris Hudspeth says the number one difference between competition chili and household chili is that there are no beans in competition chili. "If you put beans in it, it's a soup or a stew," Kris says. "I don't have time for that. Competition chili is not something you really want to make for a group of people because it is so rich and overwhelmingly powerful. It's good in small doses but in big doses, it can become overwhelming. That said, I will eat leftover competition chili because I've already spent the money for it.

"To cook a pot of competition chili I'm looking at $50: two pounds ground chuck, which is $10 right there; a can of beef broth, chicken broth, tomato sauce, tomato paste—$8; plus, all your spices and propane. Very quickly you're up to $35-$40." Kyle says that's before he's paid an entry fee, paid for gas, bought beer and whiskey, and hooked up a trailer to sleep in. He estimates that's another $100 in fees, minimum.

"You can make a pot of chili at home with household spices and whatnot, or you can get the already made recipes for $4-$5, add two pounds of ground hamburger meat, and you have a decent chili that's not real rich and heavy," he says. "Competition chili is going to sit heavy and taste heavy because you've got so many different powders and spices in there. Ultimately in competition, we are judged on one bit So that bite has to be outstanding."

Kelly Brignon

Spice company owner Kelly Brignon shares some of her tips of the trade. "When I did *Good Morning, Texas*, my top three pieces of advice were:

1) Use a quality meat. Try to get 80/20 ground chuck run through a grinder on a number two blade for a chili grind, or cube your meat—chuck tender.

2) Use fresh spices. You can make a pot of chili with spices you buy from the grocery store, and it's going to be fine. But if you want an amazing bowl of red that tastes like authentic chili, get fresh spices. Keep [them] in a cool, dry place, preferably the fridge—ground chili peppers that aren't blended with anything and don't have any preservatives—those will last six to eight months. Chili powder blends that have preservatives will last eight to twelve months. A lot of cooks put them in mason jars—airtight—they will last. You can look, smell, and taste the difference. You'll notice a difference in the quality.

3) If your chili gets too hot, do not add brown sugar. That makes it too sweet. Add tomato paste to tame the heat and give it about fifteen minutes. There is also an old wives' tale that you can use vodka to tame the heat.

"I'm a devotee of Dixon medium hot peppers. They are grown in Hatch, New Mexico. I describe it as the Cabernet of spices; it's big and juicy and beautiful. These peppers have been passed down in some instances through families and businesses. They are a high-quality chili pepper, and you won't see differences from one crop to the next. This is important since we have been in a drought. So it's nice to know that some of the peppers you buy dry or grind will be consistent. I steer my customers away from the generic New Mexico mild or California mild [peppers] because you don't know what you're getting. You're just getting what survived, and a lot of times they are grinding up everything stems, seeds, membranes, etc. A lot of customers, especially East Coast folks grow their own peppers, dry them, and grind them.
"To dry your own peppers, you can dehydrate them in the oven over a long period of time on low heat. They will dry without smoking or roasting, which will give them a differ-

ent flavor. Pull the seeds out before you grind. A lot of times people will leave membranes in for the heat and then grind that as well. Doing it for the first time, use an Anaheim or Poblano [pepper]. They are fairly mild. The last thing you want to do is put them in your food processor or grinder and get the fumes. Those fumes can knock you over. So start with one of those or a Fresno—that's a red one that looks like a jalapeño, but it's mild."

Tom Dozier

"I don't have any tricks," says Terlingua Ghostown Chili spice company owner and CASI chili cook winner Tom Dozier. "Some people add this or that. I don't ever change or switch things around." Tom swears by cooking his chili the way he always has. "I'm not cooking for myself; I'm cooking for a judge," he says. "That judge only gets one bite, so you have to make all the difference in that one bite. Competition chili is very intense; it's so strong and hot and thick. It's not good homestyle chili because it's so intense.

"Judging chili is difficult because all the flavors try to grab you. When you are cooking, you think you have to add more and more spices. But by doing that I think you are taking the chili out of chili. In the old days, people made it simple and plain. Tom's recipe reflects the plain and simple style. "Terlingua Ghostown Chili is just chili," he says.

Tom believes preparation is key to winning. "Prepare. Prepare like crazy," he says. "Luck favors the prepared, so be pre-pared."

CHILI RECIPES

"Chile" with an "e" is a pepper. "Chili" with an "i" is a dish as in chili con carne (chiles with meat). Many of the old-timers agree that original Texas-style chili contains no beans and no vegetables: chile peppers are the only exception to the rule. No tomatoes, no onions, no beans, just slow-cooked beef and spices. Other chili cooks prefer not to restrict themselves to the "no veggies, no beans" rule and play with the ingredients they love or have on hand.

In Tolbert's book *A Bowl of Red*, he mentions chili as we know it began in the late 1800s in San Antonio, Texas with a group of ladies known as the chili queens. These gals were known to light lanterns, wear roses around their chests, and otherwise lure business in with the complex aroma of their chili in the plazas of old San Antonio. In 1943, the chili queens would succumb to new laws that would no longer allow them to sell food in chili stands on the streets. The San Antonio recipes for chili lived on though, in characters such as a man named Myers whose chili drew the likes of Jesse and Frank James to his café in McKinney, Texas.

In the same way, we might judge a Tex-Mex joint by its queso; Will Rogers judged a town by its chili. "He sampled chili in hundreds of little towns, especially in Texas and Oklahoma," Tolbert reports in *A Bowl of Red*. "He kept a box score. Will finally concluded that the finest chili of his experience was in a small café in Coleman, Texas. The ingredients for this concoction included 'mountain oyster' from a bull, not a calf, raised on the slopes of the Santa Anna Mountains,' mountain oysters being a term for the testicles of an ex-bull."

Elizabeth Taylor requested that chili be shipped to her in dry ice from Texas to Rome during the filming of *Cleopatra*. Chili creates an addiction. Once you taste that one special chili, you begin to crave it. No other recipe will do. It's a dish that is both historical and mythological. And it can even open your sinuses.

Alan and Susan Dean's Chili

Courtesy of Alan and Susan Dean

Many folks on the chili trail love the Deans. They have cooked in and won several cook-offs all throughout the United States.

Makes 4 to 6 servings

2 pounds of course ground beef
1 (14.5-ounce) can of beef broth
1 (8-ounce) can of tomato sauce
1 cube of Knorr's brand beef bouillon
1 cube of Knorr's brand chicken bouillon
3 tablespoons of chili powder
1 tablespoon of granulated onion
1 tablespoon of paprika
1 packet of Sazón Goya seasoning Con Culantro Y Achiote
1 teaspoon of cayenne pepper
2 tablespoons of chili powder
1 teaspoon of granulated garlic
1 tablespoon of cumin
1/4 teaspoon of cayenne pepper
1/4 teaspoon of dark brown sugar

Brown the beef in a large pot, then cover the beef in the pot with just enough water to submerge the beef or less, to taste. Add the beef broth and the next eight ingredients through the cayenne pepper. Simmer for 1 hour.

Add the chili powder and remaining ingredients. Simmer for 20 minutes. Adjust the salt to taste and enjoy.

ALAN AND SUSAN DEAN
Written by Alan Dean

Alan and Susan Dean's fascination with competition-style chili began in 1983. Their running club chose to have a chili cook-off as a way to get members together for an evening of fun and friendship. Alan cooked a Beaumont, Texas lunch counter recipe that he got from a friend and won the cook-off. That lunch counter recipe became a favorite treat every time friends attended parties at Alan and Susan's house.

In 1991, a coworker of Susan's mentioned a sanctioned cook-off coming up on July 4. Alan and Susan packed up their ingredients, borrowed a stove, and headed off for Vienna, Virginia, where they made the finals in their first official cook-off. Over the next couple of years, the recipe was re-fined, and Alan began competing regularly in cook-offs sanctioned by the Chili Appreciation Society International (CASI).

The icon of chili cook-offs, the Terlingua International Chili Championship, is sponsored by CASI. Alan first qualified to cook in Terlingua in 1994 and has competed there every year since 1995. Susan first qualified to cook in Terlingua in 1998 and placed seventh out of 326 qualified cooks in her first try. Ten years later, Susan became the 2008 international champion of the CASI cook-off.

Alan and Susan have been winners throughout the United States, from Maine to Florida, California to Washington, Hawaii, the Virgin Islands, and places in between. They've won state championships in Massachusetts, New York, Pennsylvania, Maryland, Virginia, Colorado, Wyoming, California, and Hawaii. Television shows in Maryland, Texas, and California have featured their chili, and everyone has enjoyed their chili regardless of the locale.

Allegani Jani's Hot Pants Chili
Courtesy of Allegani Jani Schofield

This recipe won at the 1974 chili cook-off in Terlingua.

Makes 12 to 14 servings

5 pounds chuck roast, chili grind*
5 yellow onions, finely chopped (save some for on top)
2 tablespoons vegetable oil
6 cloves garlic, smashed
1 tablespoon cumin seeds
1 (28-ounce) can whole peeled tomatoes
1 can Pearl beer (or other light beer)
1 heaping tablespoon mole paste
1 teaspoon Tabasco pepper sauce
6 jalapeños, seeded and minced
1 quart of water

Spice Dump
4 ounces chili powder (I use Fiesta brand)
2 teaspoons onion powder
2 teaspoons garlic powder
2 teaspoons dried Mexican oregano
2 teaspoons sweet paprika
2 teaspoons ground cumin
1 teaspoon ground New Mexico chili pepper
1 teaspoon brown sugar
1/4 teaspoon cayenne pepper

Garnish
Cheddar cheese, shredded
Diced onions
Jalapeños
Sour cream

Season the meat with salt and pepper. Brown the meat with the onions in vegetable oil in a large cast iron pot (Dutch oven).

While the meat is browning, grind the garlic cloves and cumin seeds with a bit of water in a molcajete† (If you do not

Allegani Jani's Hot Pants Chili, continued

have a molcajete, add a little of the canned tomatoes to the garlic cloves and cumin seeds and mix them in a blender.) Then add the garlic mixture to the browning meat.

Mix all the dried seasonings for the Spice Dump together in a medium bowl.

In a blender, combine the tomatoes and the Spice Dump. Add this to the browned meat along with the beer, mole paste, Tabasco sauce, jalapeños, and water. Simmer the mixture for 2 1/2 to 3 hours or until it reaches desired thickness and texture. Make sure to stir the chili frequently. Add salt and pepper to taste.

Serve the chili hot with garnishes.

*Ask your butcher to grind your chuck roast into a chili grind. The butcher uses a different blade than the one used for ground beef resulting in meat with a coarser texture.

†A molcajete is a tool made from stone—the Mexican version of a mortar and pestle. A traditional mortar and pestle can be used.

Aoudad Chili
Courtesy of Tiffany Harelik

I spent a lot of time in Fort Davis, Alpine, Marfa and Terlingua as I was writing this book. My friend Randy Liddell in Fort Davis shared several 'unofficial' stories about his trips to the Terlingua cook-off over the years. The last day of my stay with Randy's family, he gave me an aoudad to take back to Austin so I could develop a unique chili recipe for this book. The below is the end result.

To avoid a gamey taste clean the animal properly, but you may also wish to soak the aoudad overnight before you cook with it to remove residual wild flavor. Many households have debated the best liquid for this job. Recommendations include saltwater, vinegar, buttermilk or water with lemon depending on what you have handy.

Makes 6-8 servings

2-3 tablespoons olive oil
1 white onion, diced
2-3 cloves garlic, minced
2 pounds of aoudad shoulder and backstrap, cleaned and cubed in 1/4-inch pieces
1 (8-ounce) can tomato paste
8 ounces water
2 beef bouillon cubes
1 whole jalapeño

Spice Dump
3 tablespoons chili powder
1 tablespoon ground cumin ,
1/2 teaspoon cayenne pepper
1/2 teaspoon paprika
1/2 teaspoon salt
1/2 teaspoon pepper

Garnish
Cotija cheese, crumbled
Fresh or fire roasted white onion, finely diced
Fresh or fire roasted jalapeño, finely diced
Fresh or fire roasted tomato, finely diced

Aoudad Chili, continued

Sweat the onion and garlic in a deep cast iron pot with olive oil on medium-high heat for 5 to 6 minutes or until onions become translucent. Be careful not to overcook or the garlic will burn. Add the aoudad meat to the pot with the onions and garlic. Cook approximately 10 minutes or until the meat has browned thoroughly and is no longer pink.

Add the tomato paste, water, bouillon cubes and jalapeño. Reduce heat to medium and allow the chili to simmer while you prepare the spice dump.

In a small bowl, mix all of the seasonings from the spice dump together. Pour the spice dump into the chili and allow to simmer on medium or medium-low for 30 minutes to an hour. Taste and adjust seasonings as desired. Remove chili from heat and allow it to rest 5-10 minutes before serving.

Garnish with your choice of Cotija cheese, onion, jalapeño, and tomato for a pretty red, white, and green topping.

Authentic Terlingua Chili
Courtesy of Bill Ivey

"The Original Terlingua Chili Seasoning is a product of the same spirit that inspired that very first chili cook-off," says Bill. "It is prepared and packaged by hand in the ghost town of Terlingua, Texas, and it contains all natural ingredients. Only the finest ground chile peppers, garlic, salt, and a special blend of spices are used to prepare this award-winning seasoning. Follow the directions for a delicious pot of authentic chili, or use the seasoning to wake up a pot of beans, or in soups and casseroles, or whatever your imagination or adventurous spirit may contrive." You can buy The Original Terlingua Chili Seasoning at www.ghosttowntexas.com.

Makes 2 to 4 servings

1 teaspoon bacon drippings or oil
1 pound fresh, lean ground meat (or chopped sirloin)
1/2 cup chopped onion
1 teaspoon flour
3 tablespoons of the Original Terlingua Chili Seasoning
1 (11.5-ounce) can of V8 Juice or 1 (5-ounce) can tomato purée
1 cup water

Heat the bacon drippings in a heavy pan over medium heat and add the hamburger and onion.

Sprinkle the flour over the mixture and cook, while stirring, until the onions are translucent.

Stir in the chili seasoning and cook until the meat is very lightly browned but not overcooked. Add the V8 Juice or tomato purée and water. Cover and simmer until thickened.

BILL IVEY

Bill Ivey is a second generation West Texan. His father, Rex, came to Big Bend as a pioneer trapping and buying fur. Bill grew up in Lajitas, attended grade school in Alpine and eventually Texas A & M University. Upon his return to the region, he and his father bought the town of Terlingua to preserve the buildings and culture of the ghost town. At one point, Bill ran his beer-drinking goat for mayor and the goat won. He educates the community children about Terlingua's Day of the Dead gathering to which he brings tamales and candles.

Bill began attending the Terlingua chili cook-offs in the early '70s. One of his most notable cook-off memories was meeting Hondo Crouch and other dignitaries from around the world. Eventually, Bill developed a chili seasoning which was inspired by his mother, Kitty. Bill says that Kitty was a practical, down-home cook who used plain ingredients to make spectacular meals in unconventional circumstances sometimes without electricity or running water. Bill's spice mix has won several awards at the International Fiery Foods Show. "The Original Terlingua Chili Seasoning was born out of love for Terlingua, the home to all chili cook-offs worldwide, and to the authentic, true taste of the West," says Bill.

If you're interested in any special rituals for chili making, you can take a page out of Bill's book and smudge your pot before you get started. The act of smudging clears the energy around the pot and creates space for good omens. To perform the smudge ritual, take a dried sprig or small branch of sage, and light it on one end allowing the lit end to smolder and smoke. Wave the smoke over and around your chili pot (or whatever else could use some cleansing).

Otherwise, his recipe is a straightforward basic recipe that each cook can modify to their liking. He says the thing that makes his chili so good is the use of a blend of chiles from New Mexico and impeccably fresh spices. When I ask Bill if he was in the beans or no beans camp, he says: "Absolutely not, beans are a side dish!

"The local culture of Terlingua is one of the most incredible communities that I have ever witnessed," shares Bill. "It is truly made up of people that want to live in this free-spirited, last frontier occupied by genuine people.

Big Bend Brewing Company's Unofficial Terlingua Chili
Courtesy of Mark Hinshaw and Matt Walker

This recipe from the Big Bend Brewery catering department utilizes the "beer from out here."

Makes 20 to 24 servings

4 to 6 pounds coffee-rubbed brisket, smoked and chopped (rub recipe follows)
3 whole dried guajillo chiles
3 whole dried ancho chiles
1 tablespoon dried pequin chile
1 yellow onion, chopped
1 carrot, shredded
2 jalapeños, seeded & chopped
1 habanero, seeded & chopped
4 cloves garlic, minced
1 poblano pepper, chopped
1 tablespoon olive oil
2 cans Tejas Lager, separated
1/2 (7-ounce) can pickled chipotle
1/2 pound chopped bacon
4 pounds coarse ground sirloin
2 bay leaves
2 tablespoons chili powder
2 tablespoons paprika
2 teaspoons jalapeño powder
2 teaspoons oregano
1 (14.5-ounce) can beef broth
3 tablespoons tomato paste
1 can Terlingua Golden Ale

Brisket Coffee Rub
1/2 cup dark chili powder
1/4 cup ground coffee
1/2 cup kosher salt
1/2 cup brown sugar
1/4 cup paprika
1/4 cup black pepper

Two days before preparing the chili, mix the ingredients for the rub in a large bowl. Then, generously coat the brisket with coffee rub. Wrap the meat and refrigerate overnight.

One day before preparing the chili, smoke the brisket for eight hours. Cool, chop, and refrigerate overnight.

Preheat the oven to 350 degrees F. Take the dried guajillo, ancho, and pequin chiles, and place them in a shallow pan. Roast the chiles in the oven until they puff and harden, approximately 10 minutes. Check often to avoid burning them. Remove them from the oven and let them cool. The chiles will not be hard, so you can break off the stems and empty the seeds easily. Using a small coffee or spice grinder, grind the chiles until they are processed into a powder. Depending on the degree of wetness, the ground chiles may form a paste instead of a powder. You may need to do this in batches. Set aside.

Sauté the onion, carrot, jalapeños, habanero, garlic, and poblano in olive oil for 5 minutes. Purée the sautéed vegetables with half a can of Tejas Lager. Set aside.

Purée the pickled chipotle with the other half can of Tejas Lager. Set aside.

In a 10- to 12-quart stock pot, sauté bacon over medium heat, until done but not crispy. Add the ground sirloin. Cook for 10 minutes. Add the vegetable purée and cook for an additional 10 minutes.

Add the bay leaves, chili powder, paprika, jalapeño powder and oregano and cook for 2 to 3 minutes. Add the chipotle purée and cook another 2 to 3 minutes.

Add the beef broth, tomato paste, and the golden ale, and simmer for 35 minutes. Stir in the chopped brisket. Adjust thickness, if desired, by adding more of the remaining Tejas Lager. Serve.

Big Bend Brewery
Catering Department: Mark Hinshaw and Matthew Walker

Originally from Amarillo, Mark Hinshaw now resides in Alpine, and Matt Walker, who hails from Chicago, lives in Marfa. Mark spent thirty-one years in the food and catering business in Austin before heading West, and Matt is a professional chef. They joined forces to develop the catering leg of the Big Bend Brewery.

Mark's first visit to Terlingua and the Starlight Theatre was on New Year's Eve 1999. He says the people are the thing that keeps him in the area. Matt says it's the seclusion and living off-the-grid that he loves about the area.

"My older cousin won it [the Terlingua chili cook-off] three years in a row back in the early '80s. That was the first time I heard about it," says Mark. His first year to attend was 2015. "I had to see if it lived up to the hype...it does. We went with the brewery to promote our glorious beer and make a killer chili to share with the chiliheads. We had a great time with all participants and campers. I loved seeing the big smiles from judges who tasted our chili and drank our beer: that was awesome." Mark says that the local culture is "a wonderful mix of misfits, big thinkers, and wanderers."

Matt's chili has won multiple chili cook-offs in Chicago. A few of his recipe titles include Smoked Wild Boar Chili, and White Chicken and White Bean Chili. "These were winners at Galway Bay, the best dive bar in Chicago," he says.

"Throughout my childhood, I was cooking with my mom in our kitchen. This is where I learned the basics of building flavor for a good chili. He says both the spice blend in the brewery's chili and the cooking procedures to build flavor he learned from his mom. "Remember," he says, "chili always tastes better the next day."

Mark says "a ton of smoked meat and a unique blend of chiles" are the things that make the brewery chili so good. The pair don't have any chili-making rituals yet, but "we made sure to have a Terlingua Gold or three, and so our ritual begins!" says Mark.

Matt says the best chili he ever had was at an Ice Fishing Derby in Bristol, Wisconsin. "It was a hillbilly blend that was to die for!" he says. Mark hit the nail on the head when he said, "Tasting chili is like looking at a sunset; each is beautiful, but none is ever the same. Choosing just one sunset or chili is a fool's errand." Matt says he loves making chili, loves making beer, and loves living here in the area.

Boomer's Beer Chili
Courtesy of Jennifer Boomer

"This is a quick and easy chili recipe that I love to make for potlucks," says award winning West Texas photographer Jennifer Boomer.

Makes 12 servings

5 pounds ground chuck
2 tablespoons ground coriander
2 tablespoons ground cumin
2 tablespoons olive oil
6 cloves garlic, minced
2 large yellow onions, finely chopped
2 large jalapeños with seeds, finely chopped
6 tablespoons chili powder
1 tablespoon salt
2 (15-ounce) cans tomato sauce
2 (15-ounce) cans crushed tomatoes with purée
1 (12-ounce) bottle Lagunitas IPA

Sauté the ground chuck in a large stock pot over medium-high heat until no longer pink.

In a small skillet, toast the coriander and cumin over medium heat.

Heat the oil in a large skillet over medium heat. Add the garlic, onions, and jalapeños to the oil and cook until they begin to soften.

Add the vegetable mixture to the pot with the meat. Mix in the toasted spices and chili powder. Add the salt, tomato sauce, crushed tomatoes, and beer. Bring to a boil.

Decrease heat and simmer for about 25 minutes, stirring often.

Brazilian Open Winner
Courtesy of Richard Willis

"This recipe is one that I used to win the Brazilian Open some years back," says Richard.

Makes 6 to 8 servings

1/2 pound ground pork
2 teaspoons lard, separated
2 pounds chuck roast, trimmed and ground
1 (14.5-ounce) can beef broth
1/2 (14.5-ounce) can chicken broth
1 (8-ounce) can tomato sauce
1 teaspoon white vinegar
Sharp cheddar cheese, shredded

Spice Dump #1
6 tablespoons Chimayo chile powder
1 tablespoon dried minced onion
1 tablespoon cumin
1 teaspoon garlic powder
1 teaspoon Mexican oregano
1 teaspoon paprika
3 beef bouillon cubes
1 chicken bouillon cube
1 packet Sazón Goya seasoning powder

Spice Dump #2
1 1/2 tablespoons Gebhardt's chili powder
1/2 tablespoon Adams chili powder
2 teaspoons ground cumin
1 teaspoon garlic powder
1/2 teaspoon paprika
1/2 teaspoon ground white pepper
1 beef bouillon cube
1 chipotle chile cube

Spice Kicker
1/2 teaspoon cumin
1/2 teaspoon Mexican oregano

Brown the pork in the lard and drain, and remove the meat from the pan.

Brown the chuck roast in the remaining teaspoon of lard.

Add the beef broth and 1/2 can of the chicken broth. Add the tomato sauce. Add Spice Dump #1. Boil for 30 minutes.

Add the white vinegar. Simmer for 30 minutes. Add Spice Dump #2. Simmer for 20 minutes or until the meat is tender. Stir in the shredded cheese to taste.

Rest the chili until 15 minutes before serving. Add the Spice Kicker and re-heat. Salt to taste.

RICHARD WILLIS

Originally from Akron, Ohio, Richard Willis grew up in New Orleans and moved to Texas in 1971. A retired university professor, he recalls a vacation in 1972 brought him to Terlingua for the first time. "I've being going to the cook-off for twenty-plus years," he says. Richard has placed in the top ten in many cook-offs across Texas including showmanship, chili, BBQ, beans, and peas, but he has not won at Terlingua. When volunteering at Terlingua, he stays at Cowboy Camp in his tipi. In his eyes, the cook-off culture is a "big loose family."

"Recipes continually evolve," Richard shares. "I've been cooking one thing or another for fifty-plus years. My chili recipes are from books, friends, divine intervention, maybe even satanic intervention?" When I asked if he had any special rituals or ceremonies associated with making his chili he offered: "Let it fester before you turn it in! My chili is more like the original chili. Most competition chili of today is too uniform, based on powdered ingredients, and too bland! My opinion. All the chili cooks make good chili. Well, maybe not all of them, but most make good stuff when they don't try too hard."

Carol Winkley's Ancho Chili
Courtesy of Maurine Winkley

"This is Mom's chili recipe—it's so good," shares Maurine. "It's dark in color from the ancho chiles and rich without being too heavy, which can be hard to do with chili. Making chili is a family thing, and we usually make it during the holidays. It's something that brings back a lot of nostalgia for me. My twist on the chili is to substitute brisket for the chili meat. Either cook it yourself or use leftovers from a good BBQ joint and substitute one ancho chile for two roasted hatch green chiles."

Makes 4 to 6 servings

1 cup water
2 ancho chiles (dried), seeded and deveined*
2 pounds lean ground chili beef
1 small to medium white onion, chopped
4 large (or 8 small) cloves garlic
2 (8-ounce) cans tomato sauce
2 tablespoons paprika
1 to 2 tablespoons chili powder
1 tablespoon cumin
1 teaspoon salt
2 teaspoons pepper
Garlic powder, optional
Onion powder, optional
1 heaping tablespoon masa harina
1/4 cup warm water

Garnish
Sour cream
Cotija cheese
Toasted pepitas
Cilantro

Boil a cup of water and place the chiles in the water. Let them soak for 30 to 45 minutes.

Sauté the beef until browned. Remove the meat and set aside. Add the onions to the skillet with the remaining meat juices, and cook until soft. Add the garlic and continue to sauté for 2 minutes. Add the cooked meat back into the pan with the onions and garlic.

Remove the skins from the chiles. Place the chiles and tomato sauce in a blender. Blend well. Fill each of the empty tomato sauce cans with water and set aside.

Combine the meat, onions, garlic, tomato/chile mixture, and the two cansof water in a crock pot (or a large pot).

Add the paprika, chili powder, cumin, salt and pepper to the crock pot. Add additional garlic powder and onion powder, if desired.

Cook in the crock pot on low for 8 to 10 hours, or on the stovetop on low for 2 hours.

Fifteen minutes before serving, add the masa harina to warm water and stir. Add the masa mixture to the chili and stir well.

Garnish with sour cream, Cotija cheese, toasted pepitas, and cilantro.

* To devein, remove the veins of the chiles at the same time you remove the seeds by scraping the interior walls of the chile with a spoon or knife.

MAURINE WINKLEY

"I learned to make chili from my mom and grandma," Maurine says. "They had both been making it since they were kids. They both grew up here in Texas." She says her grandma put chile pequins (tiny but hot chiles) in everything, including her chili. Maurine also says she likes to use different meats and peppers and experiment with her own chili recipes.

Come & Take It Bowl o' Red
Courtesy of Jenny Turner

"I experimented with different combinations of my favorite ingredients from winning Terlingua chili cook-off recipes plus some ingredients of my own, but the smoked, chopped brisket is what sets this chili apart," comments Jenny.

Makes 12 servings

1 tray chopped smoked brisket from Come & Take It BBQ, or 10 cups other smoked brisket
3 cups water
1/2 bottle of Shiner Bock (or other dark beer)
1 (6-ounce) can tomato paste
2 beef bouillon cubes
1 tablespoon olive oil

Spice Dump
(Mix ahead and store in a cool place for up to a month.)
4 tablespoons good quality chili powder
2 teaspoons cumin
1 tablespoon minced onion
1 teaspoon garlic powder
1 teaspoon oregano
1/2 teaspoon cayenne pepper
1/2 teaspoon red pepper
1/4 teaspoon salt

Combine all the ingredients in a stockpot with a thick bottom. Add the Spice Dump.

Simmer for 1 to 1 1/2 hours, stirring frequently to prevent burning or sticking. Add more water, as needed, to achieve the desired consistency.

JENNY TURNER

Come and Take it BBQ café owner Jenny Turner has never entered a chili competition but learned to make chili from Ken Sabe on the ghost town porch in 1993. "I wanted to make a pot of chili for this guy who had caught my eye," Jenny shares. "Ken Sabe told me the basic ingredients, plus a secret ingredient. I went home to cook the pot of chili and promptly burned it to the bottom of the pot—trying to cook over a one-burner propane camp stove was tricky! I also burned the cornbread in the small toaster oven I was using in my neighbor's apartment, as I did not have electricity at the time. The guy (now my husband) fortunately did not give up on me after that first failed chili dinner!"

Now a local bed and breakfast and restaurant owner, Jenny jokes that she has been experimenting with different recipes and talking with chili cooks about what makes excellent chili for the twenty-two years since she burnt her first attempt at the dish. The chopped smoked brisket and its unique smoky flavor make her chili stand out.

Cuban Cowgirl Chili
Courtesy of Mirt Foster

Mirt calls this "a kicky version of picadillo"—the national comfort dish of Cuba—adjusted from her mother's recipe by substituting beer for white wine. "She's hands down the best Cuban cook this side of Miami, y'all! Buen provecho!" says Mirt.

Makes 6 to 8 servings

2 tablespoons olive or canola oil
1 medium-size sweet yellow onion, chopped
1 medium-size green bell pepper, chopped
4 garlic cloves, crushed
1 small jalapeño, seeded and sliced
4 tablespoons chili powder
1 tablespoon garlic powder
2 tablespoons ground cumin
2 teaspoons pepper
2 teaspoons salt
1 (15-ounce) can tomato sauce
2 pounds lean ground beef
1 cup medium pimiento-stuffed green olives, drained and sliced in half
1/2 cup raisins
2 tablespoons of capers
3 dried whole Turkish bay leaves
2 tablespoons sugar
1 bottle Shiner Bock beer
2 cups water
2 (15-ounce) cans red kidney beans, drained and rinsed

Garnish
Sour cream or crema fresca
Fresh cilantro
Chopped, pickled jalapeños
Sliced plantains
Corn chips

In a large pot, add the oil, onion, bell pepper, fresh garlic, and jalapeño. Sauté for 5 minutes on medium heat, and add the spices: chili powder, garlic powder, ground cumin, pepper, and salt. Cook for 1 to 2 minutes until spices are fragrant, then add the tomato sauce, and simmer 5 more minutes.

Add the beef, breaking it apart until crumbly, and cook until meat is no longer pink, about 15 minutes. Decrease heat to medium-low, and add the olives, raisins, capers, bay leaves, sugar, beer, water, and beans. Cover the pot with the lid and simmer for 20 to 30 minutes.

Garnish with sour cream or crema fresca, fresh cilantro, chopped, pickled jalapeños, sliced plantain or corn chips.

MIRT FOSTER

Born in Havana, Cuba, Mirt Foster is an artist and photographer who enjoys cooking for family, friends, and the occasional movie set. A cross-country family vacation aboard an Amtrak train when Mirt was young first brought her to Terlingua. "It was a magical experience," she says. "Years later, listening to singer-songwriter Jerry Jeff Walker's ¡Viva Terlingua! record during the heyday of the cosmic cowboy pretty much sealed the Terlingua mystique." The big sky country is what keeps her coming back to Terlingua. "By day, the vast landscape let's you see for miles, and by night, the sky is filled with stars as big as, well, Texas!" shares Mirt.

Mirt has attended the cook-off as a visitor a few times since the '90s to "experience the colorful characters brought together by the notion of cooking chili in the middle of nowhere." She describes the cook-off culture as "cosmic cowboy meets stargazer chef, or two Texans walk into a bar...

"My first chili experience was at a church carnival when I was about ten years old," says Mirt. "It is my most memorable. The Ladies Club had a booth, and they made this very exotic dish called chili pie served up in these little individual Fritos bags, topped with onions, shredded cheese, and a plastic spoon. Man, this girl was hooked."

Mirt says she learned to make chili by slowly discovering American culture. "My family immigrated to the United States in the 1960s. Chili wasn't exactly on the Cuban dinner menu growing up, so when I got married, eating at my American mother-in-law's house was an ethnic experience for me. She made the best chili. Nothing fancy. Pure America. I always looked forward to dinners at her house." Mirt has a special ritual when she makes chili: "I always light a candle to my patron saints of cooking—my grandmothers. They are on cosmic speed dial, my sweet abuelitas. They look after me."

Although she has never won a Terlingua cook-off, Mirt jokes about having submitted a fancy lamb and rosemary dish to a wine magazine and winning a free subscription. "I've been making the same chili recipe, more or less, for years, always calling upon the 'ghosts of perfect chilies past' for guidance. The latest incarnation thus, culminates from a lifetime of inspired cooking, so to speak. When necessary, I take good notes."

Mirt says her chili is bold but not too hot and spicy. "The integration of savory Cuban ingredients to a rich Texas chili tradition—a melting pot if you will, of greatness—is much like the story of America and my life," shares Mirt. She says love is the most important ingredient in her chili. "Love. It's cliché, but true," she says. "Cooking is how I give to my family and how my parents gave to me. Time is important too. You can't hurry good food."

Beans or no beans for Mirt? "Beans. I'm Cuban," she says with a smile.

Dwight's Rockne Red
Courtesy of Dwight Hamilton

"The "Austin American-Statesmen" did an article on two local winners out at my ranch," says Dwight. "When it was over, they wanted my recipe. I said, 'I'm not going to give you my recipe, but I'll give you one that folks can start with.'" Dwight traveled to Port O'Connor [Texas] in January 2016, and this recipe won under another chili cook even though Dwight himself did not win anything that day. "It's won Terlingua before, and it's placed several times," he says. "One guy wins with it three to four times a year."

Makes 4 to 6 servings

1 tablespoon Crisco or lard
2 pounds ground beef, chili grind
1 (14.5-ounce) can Swanson beef broth
1 (14.5-ounce) can Swanson chicken broth
1 (8-ounce) can tomato sauce
2 serrano peppers, whole
1 jalapeño, whole

Spice Dump #1
2 tablespoons granulated onion
2 tablespoons Fiesta light chili powder
1 tablespoon Gebhardt chili powder
1 tablespoon McCormick dark chili powder
2 teaspoons beef granules
1 teaspoon chicken granules
1/2 teaspoon cayenne pepper
1/4 teaspoon season salt

Spice Dump #2
1 tablespoon Gebhardt chili powder
1 tablespoon Fiesta Light chili powder
1 teaspoon paprika
1 teaspoon cumin
1 teaspoon granulated garlic
1/2 teaspoon white pepper
1/4 teaspoon green jalapeño powder
1 packet Sazón Goya con Culantro y Achiote

Dwight's Rockne Red, continued

Spice Dump #3
1 tablespoon Gebhardt chili powder
1/2 teaspoon cumin
1/2 .teaspoon black pepper
1/2 teaspoon Hot Stuff
1/2 teaspoon brown sugar
1/4 teaspoon granulated garlic
1/4 teaspoon cayenne pepper
1/4 teaspoon salt

Melt the Crisco in a medium to large saucepan and brown the beef.

Add the beef broth, 1/2 can of the chicken broth, and the tomato sauce. Bring to a slow boil for 30 minutes.

Add Spice Dump #1. Float the serrano peppers and jalapeño on top. Cover and cook at a medium boil for 1 hour.

Remove the peppers from the mixture. Squeeze the juice of the peppers into the chili and stir. (Be careful not to spill any seeds into chili.) Add Spice Dump #2. Add the remainder of the chicken broth, as necessary, for desired consistency. Cover and cook for 30 minutes.

Add Spice Dump #3. Decrease heat to a slow boil. Cook for 20 minutes.

DWIGHT HAMILTON

Dwight Hamilton is on the board for Tolbert's Behind the Store cook-off and is president of his local chapter. He is also a member of CASI. "I cook with both groups," Dwight says. "It's a charity thing with us. Last year my group raised $65,000 for charity. It makes me feel good. Dwight says that despite the population swelling to 10,000 during the week before the chili cook-offs, it's fun to be there. "Most of the locals decide it's a good time for their vacation because the highway patrol is down there," he says.

Born in Austin, Dwight currently lives in Rockne, Texas. He makes a living doing mobile home sales and service. "My first trip to Terlingua was a guy-only road trip in 1995," shares Dwight. "The Original Terlingua International Championship Chili Cook-off and the chilihead camaraderie are what keeps me going back."

He has won too many individual cook-offs to mention. "I've placed in Terlingua a couple of times, placing fourth one year and third another," Dwight shares. "I learned to make chili through good friends providing me with a basic recipe in 1995. Although not featured in print publications, my recipe appears on the website *CentralTexasChili.com* on the "Recipes, Tips & Tricks" page.

"How long did it take me to develop my recipe? From that initial basic recipe, it took me approximately twelve years to finish tweaking it." He partially attributes a good blend of spices to the success of his chili recipe, but he says the most important ingredient is the meat. "Aside from my own chili, Mike 'BB' Hughes made the best chili," says Dwight. "He was the world champion in 2007 and passed away on his way home from Terlingua in November 2008."

Eatin' Chili
Courtesy of Richard Willis

"Eatin' Chili is what I cook for home consumption," says Richard. "Competition chili is great one spoonful at a time but probably not for a whole bowlful." Richard gives you a few tips to get you started:

Get lean round steak, sirloin, etc. —the better the meat, the better the chili. Have the butcher coarse grind it for chili. If you use hamburger grind, you'll get a mess. If they won't grind it and you don't have a meat grinder, it can be cut into 1/4-inch (tiny) cubes. Some of the competitions require cut rather than ground meat.

The ground chili pepper should be available in the spice section. Chili powder can be substituted, but it usually contains cumin and garlic powder in addition to chili peppers. Those ingredients should be cut back a little if you use chili powder. For the onion, pick a Texas 1015 or a Georgia Vidalia.

Be sure to use Mexican oregano, not Italian oregano: it's a different plant.

Chili petines: if you can't find these just up the cayenne to suit your taste.

Masa harina is a thickening agent; it is basically corn flour. Cinnamon: many cooks will add a just a taste. It adds a little mysterious tang but doesn't make the chili taste like cinnamon.

Chipotle peppers are smoked and cured jalapeños. They are usually quite hot and add a smoky taste to the chili. They'll be in the canned food section, and a little goes a long way. Beans—only Yankees put beans in chili. They shoot you, then hang you, then burn the body, in Texas, for such vile behavior.

Note on peppers: The ground chili pepper and the poblanos are not very hot. They give a little heat but mostly they give flavor and color. Cayenne and chili petines give "up front heat" i.e., they give that initial fire. If you like "front heat" add a little black pepper, say 1/4 teaspoon, when you add the cayenne. The jalapeños and chipotles give "after heat", i.e. they hit the tongue on a delay, usually just after you swallow."

Makes 4 to 6 servings

2 pounds lean round steak or sirloin, chili grind or cut into 1/4-inch cubes
1 to 2 teaspoons olive oil
1 white onion, chopped
3 poblano peppers, skinned* seeded and chopped
3 garlic cloves, minced (or substitute 1 to 2 tablespoons garlic powder)
1/3 cup chili powder
1 (8-ounce) can tomato sauce
1 beer, dark
Chipotle peppers (optional, 2 or 3 to taste)
2 tablespoons comino (or powdered cumin)
1 teaspoon Mexican oregano
1/4 teaspoon paprika
Cayenne pepper
Dash of cinnamon (optional)
2 beef bouillon cubes
3 jalapeños
5-6 chili petines
Salt and pepper
Masa harina (optional)
Beans (optional)

Garnish
1-2 cups cheddar cheese, grated

In a large chili pot, brown the beef, drain the grease, and remove the meat from the pot.

Next, sauté the onion, poblanos, and garlic in the olive oil in the same pot that the meat was cooked in. Add the meat back into the pot. Then add the chili powder. Mix well. Add the tomato sauce, beer, and chipotle peppers. Stir to combine.

Eatin' Chili, continued

Stir the comino, Mexican oregano, and paprika into the pot. Add cayenne to taste, and the dash of cinnamon. Stir to combine well. Crush the bouillon cubes and add them. With a sharp knife, make a few slits along the sides of the jalapeños, and place them whole into the pot. Add the chili petines.

Cover and bring to a boil for about 5 minutes, then simmer at least 30 to 45 minutes. Don't open the lid unnecessarily; this can cause the spices and oils to escape impacting the flavor. Turn off the heat and let the chili rest for 30 minutes.

Remove the jalapeños, squeeze them gently over the pot to add their juice and either discard them or remove their seeds and stems, chop them up and add them back into the pot. Adjust salt, pepper, and heat to taste.

If the chili is not thick enough, add the masa harina and cook for another 10-15 minutes, or mix in cheddar cheese to thicken.

*Directions for skinning poblanos

Skinning and seeding poblano peppers can be accomplished most easily by cutting off the tops and removing the seeds and associated membranes.

Preheat the oven to 500 degrees F. Spray a pizza pan with PAM and stand the peppers upside down, placing the tops next to them. Roast them in the oven for 10 minutes or so until the skin has puffed away from the pepper. Take the peppers from the oven, pop them into a Ziploc bag, and put them in the freezer for 10 minutes. The skins will slip right off. You can also roast them over the burner if you have a gas stove, and then peel the skins off.

Ghostown Chili

Courtesy of Deanna Castillo

Deanna credits Roger Foltz and Tom Dozier for helping her develop this award-winning recipe, which she also serves at High Sierra Bar and Grill in Terlingua, Texas.

Makes 4-6 servings

2 pounds of beef chili grind
1 (14.5-ounce) can beef broth
1 (14.5-ounce) can chicken broth
1 (8-ounce) can tomato sauce
2 serrano peppers, whole
Salt as needed

Spice Dump #1
1 tablespoon Mild Bill's Cowtown light chili powder
1 tablespoon Mild Bill's San Antonio original chili powder
1 tablespoon Mild Bill's Dixon medium hot chili powder
2 teaspoons Mild Bill's onion granules
2 teaspoons Wyler's beef granules
2 teaspoons Wyler's chicken granules
1 1/2 teaspoons Mild Bill's garlic granules
1/4 teaspoon Mild Bill's cayenne pepper
1/8 teaspoon kosher salt

Spice Dump #2
1 tablespoon Mild Bill's cumin
1 tablespoon Mild Bill's San Antonio original chili powder
1 tablespoon Mexene chili powder (available from Mild Bill's)
1 tablespoon Mild Bill's Cowtown light chili powder
1/2 teaspoon Gunpowder Foods Hot Stuff (available from Mild Bill's)
1/8 teaspoon Mild Bill's cayenne pepper
1/8 teaspoon brown sugar
1 package Sazón Goya (available from Mild Bill's)

Brown the beef in a large pot; drain the grease and remove the meat from the pot. Add the beef broth, chicken broth, and tomato sauce in the same pot used for the meat; bring to a boil.

Ghostown Chili, continued

Once boiling, add the serrano peppers and Spice Dump #1. Add the meat back into the pot. Boil on medium heat for 30 to 35 minutes or until meat is done. Squeeze the juice of the peppers into the chili and discard the peppers.

Forty-five minutes before serving, bring the chili to a boil. Add Spice Dump #2, and cook for 30 minutes over medium-low to medium heat. Check for salt, and adjust, if necessary.

Herman and Deanna's Ft. Stockton Mule Deer Chili

Courtesy of Deanna Castillo

Deanna and her husband Herman Everett own the High Sierra Bar and Grill in Terlingua, Texas which is part of the El Dorado Hotel. While Deanna is a woman of distinction on the chili trail, Herman is an excellent cook in his own right having one of the best bean recipes in West Texas. The couple developed this recipe to use the meat from one of Herman's hunting trips with his family.

Makes 6-8 servings

2 to 2 1/2 pounds of venison
1/4 cup cooking oil
1/2 cup white onion, chopped
3 cloves garlic, minced
1 (8-ounce) tomato sauce
1 (14.5-ounce) can beef broth
8 ounces water

Spice Dump
4 tablespoons chili powder
2 tablespoon light chili powder
1 tablespoon ground cumin
2 teaspoons granulated onion and garlic
1/2 teaspoon cayenne pepper
1/2 teaspoon salt

Brown the venison over medium-high heat in a 3-to 4-quart pot with the cooking oil, chopped onion, and minced garlic until the meat is cooked.

Next add the tomato sauce, beef broth, and water. Increase the heat and bring to a boil. Add the chili mix. Turn heat down to medium and simmer 30 minutes.

Turn off heat. Rest for 5 minutes before serving. Serve with your favorite topping.

Judy's Mild and Tentative Chili
Courtesy of Judy Alter

Judy wrote "Texas Is Chili Country: A Brief History with Recipes." This is her personal recipe. She says her family likes to top it with chopped purple onion and grated cheddar.

Makes 2-4 servings

1 large onion, chopped
1 clove garlic, chopped
1 to 2 tablespoons oil, or enough oil to sauté onion, garlic, and beef
1 pound ground beef
1 (8-ounce) can tomato sauce
1 cup beer
4 teaspoons chili powder
2 teaspoons salt
1/2 teaspoon Tabasco sauce
2 cups beans

Sauté the onion and garlic until lightly browned in the oil; add hamburger and cook approximately 6-8 minutes or more until the meat is no longer pink.

Add the tomato sauce, beer, chili powder, salt and the Tabasco sauce. Simmer for 60 to 90 minutes. Stir occasionally, and add more beer, as needed for desired consistency. Taste the chili and add more chili powder, as desired.

Add the beans, and heat just before serving.

JUDY ALTER
Originally from Chicago, Judy Alter now lives in Fort Worth and is a full-time writer. "I'm retired as Director of TCU [Texas Christian University] Press and am an author writing mysteries," she says. Judy also comments that she writes some history and food books too.

She falls among the chili lovers who approve of beans but says she has never been to Terlingua. She learned to make her chili "by guess and by gosh." Judy also includes this recipe in her cookbook and memoir, *Cooking My Way Through Life with Kids and Books.* She says that it's the addition of beer that makes her chili so good.

Kelly Brignon's 2010 TICC Winning Chili Recipe
Courtesy of Kelly Brignon

Kelly started cooking chili in 2002 and bought Mild Bill's
Spice company in 2009. This is her award-winning recipe.

Makes 4 to 6 servings

2 pounds of beef, chili grind
1 (14.5 ounce) can beef broth
1 (14.5 ounce) can chicken broth
1 (8-ounce) can tomato sauce
2 serrano peppers, whole

Spice Dump #1
2 tablespoon Mild Bill's Dixon medium hot chili powder
1 tablespoon Mild Bill's Cowtown light chili powder
2 teaspoons onion granules
2 teaspoons beef granules
2 teaspoons chicken granules
1/2 teaspoon cayenne
1/8 teaspoon salt
1/8 teaspoon Tellicherry* pepper

Spice Dump #2
3 tablespoons Mild Bill's San Antonio original chili powder
1 tablespoon Mild Bill's Cowtown light chili powder
1 tablespoon cumin
2 1/4 teaspoons garlic
1/8 teaspoon Terlingua Dust
1/8 teaspoon white pepper
1/8 teaspoon cayenne
1/8 teaspoon brown sugar
1 package Sazón Goya seasoning packet

Brown the beef in a large pot; drain the grease and remove
the meat from the pot.

Add the beef broth, chicken broth, and tomato sauce; bring
to a boil. Once boiling, add the serrano peppers, Spice Dump
#1, and the beef. Reduce heat to medium for 30-35 minutes
and cook on a low boil until the meat is done.

Kelly Brignon's 2010 TICC Winning Chili Recipe, continued

Squeeze juices from the peppers into the chili, and then discard the peppers.

Forty-five minutes before serving, bring the chili to a high rolling boil. Add Spice Dump #2, and cook for 30 minutes over medium-low to medium heat. Adjust salt to taste.

*Tellicherry peppercorns are left on the vine longer developing a deep, rich flavor. This type of pepper is considered the finest pepper in the world.

Mild Bill's Chili Verde
Courtesy of Kelly Brignon

Makes 4 to 6 servings

1 tablespoon salt
3 tablespoons ground cumin
2 tablespoons green chili powder
1 tablespoon Spice Mistress green chili powder
1/4 teaspoon dried oregano
5 jalapeños, seeded
8 ounces Santa Cruz green chile paste
2 pounds pork loin, cubed
2 (14.5-ounce) cans chicken broth
1 cup water, plus 1 other cup
1 medium sweet onion, chopped
2 cloves garlic
1 (28-ounce) can whole green chiles, seeded and diced

In a small bowl, mix together the salt, cumin, green chili powders and oregano; set them aside.

In another small bowl, blend the jalapeños and the green chile paste together; set that aside.

Brown the pork in a frying pan and set aside.

Combine the chicken broth, first cup of water, onion, and the garlic in a pot. Heat until the onion is translucent. Add the blended jalapeños, cooked pork and 1 1/2 tablespoons of cumin mixture to the pot. Continue cooking over medium heat.

After 1 hour, add 1/3 can of the green chiles, and another 1 1/2 tablespoons of cumin mixture, and blend together until smooth in a blender. Add the blended mixture to the pot.

After 2 1/2 hours, add the remaining canned green chiles, the green chile paste, and cumin mixture. Salt to taste. Add additional water, if needed, for desired consistency.

Mild Bill's Competition Chili Recipe
Courtesy of Kelly Brignon

Kelly of Mild Bill's Spice company shares one more recipe.

Makes 4-6 servings

2 pounds beef, chili grind
1 (14.5-ounce) can Swanson beef broth
1 (14.5-ounce) can Swanson reduced sodium chicken broth
1 (8-ounce) can Hunt's tomato sauce, no salt added
2 serrano peppers

Spice Dump #1
1 tablespoon Cowtown light chili powder
1 tablespoon EC Special chili powder
1 tablespoon San Antonio Original chili powder
2 1/2 teaspoons New Mexico chili powder (hot or mild)
2 teaspoons onion granules
2 teaspoons garlic granules
2 teaspoons Wyler's beef granules
2 teaspoons Wyler's chicken granules
1/2 teaspoon cayenne
1/8 teaspoon salt

Spice Dump #2
2 tablespoons San Antonio Original chili powder
1 tablespoon cumin
1 tablespoon EC Special chili powder
1/4 teaspoon Hot Stuff
1/4 teaspoons brown sugar
1 package Sazón Goya seasoning packet

Brown the meat in a large pot and drain it well. Set cooked meat aside. Wipe the pot clean and add all of the beef broth, 1/2 of the chicken broth, and all of the tomato sauce. Prick holes in the serrano peppers and drop them into the liquid. Once it reaches a boil, add Spice Dump #1.

Let the spices, liquid and serrano peppers boil for 5-6 minutes, and then add the meat back in. Cook on a medium boil for 30 to 45 minutes (or until meat is done). Remove the peppers and squeeze the juices into the chili.

Turn off the heat and let the chili rest for 20 minutes. Reheat the chili and let it come to a boil. Add Spice Dump #2.

Decrease the heat to medium-high and continue to cook at a steady boil. Cook for 15 minutes. Add the remaining chicken broth to desired thickness. Add salt to taste. Continue cooking for 10 more minutes. Adjust any additional seasonings to taste and serve.

KELLY BRIGNON

"I started cooking chili in 2002 with Kary Fieseler and Sherree Nichols," says Kelly Brignon about her lifelong friends. "When we first started cooking, we were like sponges. We absorbed EVERYTHING. If you had told us you put dog doo doo in your chili and had just won first place—well, guess what we would have done? You name it; we tried it."

Kelly says she and her friends even tried McDonald's ketchup packets, butter, and grease reserved from cooked, drained meat. They tried anything and everything. "We were so green and so new, and we just wanted to place. We had fun whether we were winners or losers," she says. "We'd go home and on Monday, the emails between us would start flying. Where were we cooking next? What food were we going to bring? What recipe were we going to cook? What new tip had we heard while we were at our last cook-off?

"We all started cooking Bob Coats's recipe. From there we branched out, and each tried our own thing with varying degrees of success. I was not the best student of chili cooking. I constantly forgot stuff necessary for cooking (propane, anyone?), regularly forgot to put my dumps in when I was supposed to, and was just a general screw-up. I was more interested in cooking beans (and doing quite well) and sitting in my chair and reading magazines, and discussing what food we were all going to bring to our next chili cook-off. For Kary and me, feeding people is essential, so we used chili cook-offs as a means to feed the masses.

"I got pregnant in June 2003 and didn't cook chili for a few years. I was eager to start cooking again and just like before, hooked up with Kary and Sherree and got back to cooking chili. This time, I was a little more interested in doing well, so I made sure I brought the necessities and paid better attention to what I was doing. It seemed now that I cared more about what I was doing, the harder it was to get a point. I got points before cooking some pretty crappy chili...so I was pissed that I couldn't 'buy' a point cooking a decent pot of chili! In fact, I went from October of 2005 to March of 2006 without one point, and that was cooking every weekend— usually Saturday and Sunday. I SUCKED!

"So, I did what any sane person would do...I spent hours researching chili recipes, chili powder blends, and ground chili peppers and decided that Bob's 1999 recipe that I had started out using, in the beginning, was what I needed to go back to in order to get my points and qualify. I cooked the recipe exactly as it was written. I did not deviate from it. I learned that recipe inside and out. I knew how it tasted after each dump, how it tasted after it had sat in a Styrofoam cup for twenty minutes, and I knew what it tasted like the next day. I was relentless! It paid off because I got my points and qualified for Terlingua. We didn't go in 2006, but I knew I was on track to qualify again for 2007 and that my husband and I would be making the trip to the desert.

"I kept cooking Bob's recipe, and once I qualified for TICC 2007, I started playing around. I ordered every available chili powder and ground chili pepper from Mild Bill's and Pendery's. I cooked a pot of chili at least two or three nights a week. I was obsessed!" Kelly says if one of her weeknight recipes tasted good in a Styrofoam cup (just like it would at the judge's table), then that would be the recipe she chose to cook for the upcoming weekend's competition. "I rarely cooked the same recipe twice," she says. "I did, however, come up with a base recipe and cooked it the majority of the time. I managed to get a lot of points cooking it. It's the recipe that led me to "Champ" (aka Tom Dozier).

"After placing second at Traders Village [a non-sanctioned cook-off in Grand Prairie, Texas], Tom came up to me and asked to taste my chili. I obliged, and we struck up a conversation. He was excited to meet someone from Waxahachie (where he grew up), and he was also looking for help with cooking competition chili. We exchanged phone numbers and started communicating on, literally, a daily basis. I gave him his first recipe in April 2008 (just a good base recipe to get started), and he cooked it until December when I gave him my recipe. Tom placed first (his best finish ever) the Sunday after the Doe's Chili Cook-off at the Irving Elks Lodge. That qualified him for Terlingua, and I told him to keep cooking that recipe. I got second that day. He beat me with my own recipe.

"Tom kicked ass with that recipe and went to his first TICC in 2009. I don't think he made it out of the first round. But Tom is a competitor, and he was determined to win. Tom came back to Irving with a plan—he was going to win TICC, and he knew he had the recipe to help him do it. For the next year, Tom cooked almost every weekend and won constantly. Tom always texts me his [competition] number so that I know what number to listen for when the judges start announcing winners." In 2010, Tom won his first TICC championship. Kelly says as soon as Boomer called out the first place winner, she recognized Tom's number.

"I cannot express how excited I was that day, not just because that was my recipe, but more importantly because my friend had won. Tom is the absolute embodiment of a competitive chili cook. He wants to win; he expects to win, and he gets pissed if he doesn't. Kelly says riding home with first-place-winner Tom and her husband (who'd only won eighth place) was the longest ride home ever. "And to Tom's credit, he took T.J. Cannon under his wing and paid it forward. I couldn't be more proud of both of them and their accomplishments.

"I like to cook chili, and as long as I place, I'm happy." Kelly says over the past few years that helping people win is the thing she enjoys most of all. "Winning for me is a double-edged sword," she says. "If I do win, some people think I have an unfair advantage because I own a spice company. If I don't win, then who would want to buy spices from a loser?

"I like that I have been able to cook when I want, qualify easily, and then pick and choose where I cook after I've qualified. I have never placed at TICC—but my recipe has. My husband, Gary, placed eighth the same year Tom won. I made it to pre-finals." Kelly likes to tell both of them that had she gotten into the finals that year, her chili would have kicked both of their asses!

"I am the 2009 Tri-State Open Chili Champion and the 2011 State Fair of Texas winner," she says. "I've won and placed at many other cook-offs since I started cooking chili on a regular basis. My husband is the 2013 Texas Men's State Champion." With good reason she's very pleased with the recipe that Tom, her husband Gary, and countless others have used and placed well. "It makes me feel good about what I do and what I can to contribute to CASI.

"I know a lot of chili cooks who would sooner quit cooking chili rather than help out a new cook with a solid recipe. I don't have time for people like that. If you think that giving someone a real recipe is going to decrease your chances of getting points; then you take chili way too seriously. I've seen recipes given to new cooks that either don't have all of the ingredients in them, or they tell them to use some crazy stuff that you would never put in chili. And then what happens? Those new cooks are discouraged, and they quit cooking. And those long-time cooks who were 'helping' them out? They keep complaining that there aren't enough new chili cooks to keep CASI from dying.

One of the recipes Kelly contributed is the 2010 TICC winning recipe. Kelly says that she, Gary, and Tom have placed with it numerous times over the years, including a first-place win at 2011 Tri-State Open Chili Championship. "It's a good recipe," she says. "It's my recipe, and I'm proud of it. Are you going to start cooking it and win TICC in 2014? Hell, if I know! But, I do know that you can take this recipe and adjust it for what works best for you and for your area.

"Each part of the country does something a little different when cooking competition chili. The base is pretty much the same. It's the little secrets and tweaks that make chili recipes unique to different parts of the country.

"I don't care that I'm not the one holding the big pepper. I feel good knowing that I've contributed to not only Tom and my husband getting on stage, but a lot of other folks as well. To me, that's what cooking CASI chili is really about. I am blessed to own a spice business and be able to get to know chili cooks all over the country and the world. I always want to be someone who can be trusted to help out a chili cook—new or old—whether they need a new recipe to get them started or need a good one tweaked to get them back on track. Since I started cooking chili, I've been able to help someone new become a force to be reckoned with, as well as help a long-time cook (Dr. Ray Calhoun) get back on track and qualify for TICC before his passing this past spring. That, to me, is the meaning of cooking chili."

Kelly and Gary bought Mild Bill's Spice company in 2009. "When we started cooking competition chili in the early 2000s we bought our spices from Henry's (the other spice company). As we started cooking more, we kept hearing the name Mild Bill's so we started ordering from them. That's how I met Bill and Tamara Dees. Tamara and I just bonded over spices. I would email her a lot if I had questions or if I was trying new products she was putting out.

"We heard that they had put it [Mild Bill's] up for sale. I looked at my husband and was like 'we have to do this.' Looking back, I would do it all over again. It was not a sound business decision; it was made from the heart. I love spices. I love to cook. I was so involved in chili we just had to have it. We approached Bill and Tamara and purchased the business from them in 2009.

"My husband, Gary cooks a lot more than I do now. We have an active daughter, so I'm doing more mom stuff. But we stay active and keep the line of communication open with our customers. We want to be seen and be available, and people relate to that. If they have questions or need help, we stay visible and help. We sponsor the Texas Lady's State Chili Championship Cook-Off, which is an automatic qualifier. We sponsor men's state. We inherited those (sponsorships) when we bought Mild Bill's."

Those are only a few of the plethora of cook-offs Mild Bill's sponsors. Kelly and her husband cook in Terlingua too—at all three factions of the chili competitions: Tolbert's, CASI and ICS. To all the chili cooks out there, Kelly says, "Good luck—and keep it spicy!"

Pedernales River Chili

President and Lady Bird Johnson's recipe
Reprinted from *A Bowl of Red* by Frank X. Tolbert by permission of the Texas A&M University Press

Mrs. Lady Bird Johnson was said to have had "chili pangs" for President Lyndon Johnson's "Pedernales River Chili" and had cards printed with their chili recipe. "It has been almost as popular as the government pamphlet on the care and feeding of children," she wrote.

Makes 12 servings

4 pounds of chili meat (venison or lean beef)
1 large chopped onion
2 cloves of garlic
1 teaspoon of oregano (Spanish for the wild marjoram, which grows in Texas)
1 teaspoon of ground cumin seeds
6 teaspoons of chili powder (or more if you want it warmly flavored)
2 16-ounce cans of tomatoes
salt to suit you
2 cups of hot water

Put the meat, the onion, and the garlic cloves, which have been finely chopped, in a large skillet and sear until grayish. Add the rest of the ingredients, bring to a boil, lower the heat, and simmer for an hour with the cover on the skillet. Skim off the grease.

*Mexican oregano is a type of wild marjoram that grows in Texas. Dried marjoram or dried verbena may be substituted.

Pork and Black Bean Chili
Courtesy of Mirt Foster

"A classic flavor combo and the addition of espresso guaran-tees your taste buds will want to wake up and salsa dance! Si Señor, Baila Conmigo!" says the Cuban cowgirl Mirt Foster.

Makes 6 to 8 servings

3 tablespoons olive or canola oil
2 pounds of lean, boneless pork
sirloin chops, cut into small pieces
1 medium sweet yellow onion, chopped
1 medium green bell pepper, chopped
4 cloves garlic, crushed
2 tablespoons chili powder
1 tablespoon garlic powder
2 tablespoons ground cumin
1 teaspoon dried oregano
1 teaspoon pepper
2 tablespoons sugar
2 teaspoons salt
4 cups water
1 (15-ounce) can tomato sauce
1 (15-ounce) can Rotel diced tomatoes with diced green chiles, undrained
2 (15-ounce) cans black beans, drained, rinsed
2 tablespoons dried espresso powder

Garnish
Sour cream or crema fresca
Fresh cilantro, chopped
1 lime, sliced into wedges

In a large pot, add oil and pork; stir the meat while cooking on medium heat until browned, about 15 minutes. Add the onion, bell pepper, fresh garlic, and cook for 5 minutes.

Add the chili powder, garlic powder, cumin, oregano, pepper, sugar, salt, and heat until fragrant, approximately 3 minutes. Add the water. Cover with a lid, bring to a low boil, and cook for 45 minutes or until meat is very tender.

Decrease the heat to medium-low, add the tomato sauce, diced tomatoes and chiles, the black beans, and the espresso powder. Simmer for 20 minutes.

Garnish with sour cream or crema fresca, fresh cilantro, and a lime wedge.

Rockne Red Chili
Courtesy of Richard Willis

"This recipe was originally developed by Dwight Hamilton and is the basis of many current competition recipes," says Richard. "Remember, a recipe is a guideline. A good cook tweaks a recipe to suit his/her tastes. Also, never trust what a chili cook says about his/her recipe!!! Mine are factual, but I don't have secrets. Too old for that!"

Makes 4 to 6 servings

2 pounds ground chuck
1 tablespoon Crisco or other lard
1 (14.5-ounce) can Swanson beef broth
1/2 (14.5-ounce) can Swanson chicken broth
1 (8-ounce) can tomato sauce
2 serrano peppers, whole
1 jalapeño, whole

Spice Dump #1
1 tablespoon Gebhardt chili powder
2 tablespoons Fiesta light chili powder
1 tablespoon McCormick dark chili powder
2 teaspoons granulated onion
2 teaspoons beef bouillon granules
1 teaspoon onion powder
1 teaspoon chicken bouillon granules
1/2 teaspoon cayenne
1/4 teaspoon season salt

Spice Dump #2
1 tablespoon Gebhardt chili powder
1 tablespoon Fiesta light chili powder
2 teaspoons ground cumin
2 teaspoons granulated garlic
1/2 teaspoon ground white pepper
1/4 teaspoon green jalapeño powder
1 packet Sazón Goya seasoning (orange packet)

Spice Dump #3
1 tablespoon Gebhardt chili powder
1 teaspoon ground cumin

Rockne Red Chili, continued

1/2 teaspoon ground black pepper
1/2 teaspoon Hot Stuff
1/4 teaspoon granulated garlic
1/4 teaspoon cayenne
1/4 teaspoon salt
1/4 teaspoon brown sugar

Brown the ground chuck in the Crisco or lard in a 4-quart pot. Add the beef broth, chicken broth, and tomato sauce. Cut slits in the serrano peppers and the jalapeño. Float the whole peppers on top of the mixture. Cover and boil slowly for 30 minutes.

Add Spice Dump #1. Cover and boil on medium for 1 hour. Remove the floating peppers and squeeze the juices into the pot taking care not to add the seeds.

Add Spice Dump #2. Cover and simmer for 30 minutes.

Add Spice Dump #3. Cover and cook on a low simmer for 20 minutes more.

Roger Foltz's Championship Chili
Courtesy of Roger Foltz

"This recipe calls for light and dark chili powders," says award-winning chili cook Roger Foltz. "This refers essentially just to the color and has nothing to do with the heat."

Makes 4 to 6 servings

2 pounds ground chuck
1 tablespoon Crisco
1 (15-ounce) can beef broth
1 (12-ounce) can tomato sauce
1 (15-ounce) can chicken broth

Spice Dump #1
1 tablespoon paprika
1 tablespoon garlic powder
1 tablespoon onion powder
1 tablespoon beef bouillon
1 tablespoon chicken bouillon

Spice Dump #2
1/2 teaspoon salt
1/2 teaspoon brown sugar
1/4 teaspoon jalapeño powder
1/4 teaspoon coriander (also known as cumin)
1/4 teaspoon oregano
1 packet Sazón Goya seasoning

Spice Dump #3
2 tablespoons Pueblo dark chili powder
1 tablespoon paprika
1 tablespoon Fort Worth light chili powder
1/4 teaspoon white pepper
1/8 teaspoon red pepper
1/8 teaspoon ancho chile powder
1/8 teaspoon habanero powder

Spice Dump #4
2 tablespoons Rancho dark chili powder
1 tablespoon San Antonio red chili powder

Roger Foltz's Championship Chili, continued

1 tablespoon cumin
1 teaspoon paprika
1 teaspoon MSG
1/4 teaspoon brown sugar

In a large chili pot, brown the ground chuck in the Crisco and drain the grease. Return the meat to the chili pot and add the beef broth and tomato sauce. Add the chicken broth to desired consistency, and bring to boil.

Add Spice Dump #1. Decrease the heat to a simmer and cook 1 hour for meat chunks and about 15 minutes less for ground meat.

Add Spice Dump #2. Cook for 30 minutes.

Add Spice Dump #3. Cook for 10 minutes and then turn the heat off.

Thirty minutes before competition turn-in time (or serving), reheat chili.

Ten minutes before turn-in time (or serving), add Spice Dump #4. Adjust salt and heat to taste.

ROGER FOLTZ

The first time Roger cooked at CASI, he won it. "That's a fun thing to claim," says Roger. "Debbie Ashland and Larry Walton also won their first time cooking at CASI. We tell first-time cooks every year down there that they can do it too because several of us have." But that's not the only chili cook-off where he placed that day.

Roger joined several friends at the championship chili cook-off in Terlingua, in 1998. "They had earned the required points to cook in the event, and I was going just as a spectator and to work in the Faded Love Chili Company show team down at Tolbert's. Our motto was: 'My wife ran off with my best friend, and I miss him.'

"After attending Tolbert's in Terlingua, I decided I would try my hand at cooking the state dish of Texas and earned qualification to cook in their championship the following year and every year since then.

"Two chili groups hold their championship in Terlingua on the first Saturday in November each year: Chili Appreciation Society International (CASI) and the Tolbert Behind the Store group. Living in Dallas, several friends in the chili community who were involved in CASI challenged me to 'come cook with the big boys' at their event. I didn't want to abandon my friend's at Tolbert's, so in 2004 I cooked both contests.

"Starting at 3 a.m. over at the Tolbert's site I got my chili where I wanted it, turned it off, and put it on the floor board of my buddy Joe's car. I asked him to put the chili back on forty-five minutes before turn in, and put it in the [judges' tasting] cups and turn it in. I then went to the CASI site at 8 a.m. I used the same recipe. It's one I got from Billy Cudd, a Tolbert cook.

"I was certainly not the first to cook both events the same day, and not the first to place in both events the same day, but I was the first to win the CASI event with 337 cooks, and place second in the Tolbert event with ninety-seven cooks on the same day. I was also on the first-place large show team at the CASI cook-off that day."

Roger says that the good Lord looked kindly on him that day in November and that he felt very, very blessed to do so well in both competitions. "Let me give credit to John Billy Murray," he continues. "He was the first person to place in both of them on the same day. He wasn't in the top three in either one but the first to place both the same day in 1988. He won eighth at CASI and tenth at Tolbert's. "I was on stage at CASI after winning," Roger remembers, "and this lady came over and said 'They're mad at you over at Tolbert's. You're second over there.'" Roger lost the first place win at Tolbert's by only one point.

"In 2008, I was elected to the CASI Board of Directors and served as secretary until 2013," he shares. "During the year, CASI sanctions approximately 600 chili cook-offs in the United States, Mexico, and the Virgin Islands. Those events raise approximately $1.5 million for various charities—both national and local charities. CASI also awards scholarships to deserving students across the US. "I have always loved to cook and try new recipes. I even took cooking in high school and Foods and Nutrition in college at Texas Tech."

To date, Roger has cooked chili in twenty-three different states, including Alaska and Hawaii. He has also cooked in San Miguel, Mexico, and the Virgin Islands. "There's only one person in ICS that has cooked in all fifty states: Wes Carlson," Roger shares.

Roger has cooked with The Faded Love Chili Company for over twenty years. "We came from a group that first visited Terlingua and the chili championship in 1990 to experience a memorable time with good friends," shares Roger.

"All of the original members of Faded Love Chili Company worked together at a bank in Birmingham, Alabama in the early 1970s. Over the years, we kept it in the family. We added brothers and sons, neighbors, and Boy Scout buddies. We were all friends and friends of friends. In 2000, we added Dr. Ted Hume and several of his long time chili-cooking buddies from college."

In 2000, Faded Love was the first group awarded the Lifetime Achievement Award for service to the Original Terlingua International Chili Cookoff (OTICC). "We are still just a bunch of friends who enjoy dark whiskey, a good cigar, and the beauty of a Terlingua sunset," shares Roger who is a lifetime CASI member.

Starlight Theatre Chili

Courtesy of Diego Palacios of the Starlight Theatre

This large batch quantity is exactly how the Starlight prepares chili for the restaurant today. Serve with tortilla chips or saltines.

Makes 14 to 16 servings

13 pounds ground beef
2 white onions
6 tomatoes
5 jalapeños
14 ounces ancho chiles, dried
1 (12-ounce) can tomato sauce
1/2 cup garlic powder
3/4 cup cumin
6 bay leaves
1/3 cup salt

Brown the beef and drain the grease. Char the onions, tomatoes, and jalapeños until the skins have started to blacken on a flattop grill or in a cast iron skillet and purée.

In a separate pot, submerge the ancho chiles in water, and bring them to a boil. Drain them. Purée chiles in a food processor and slowly add water until you have reached a thin consistency. Add the ancho purée, charred vegetables, tomato sauce, garlic powder, cumin, bay leaves and salt to the pot with the meat. Bring to a simmer and cook for 30 minutes.

DIEGO PALACIOS

Born in Chicago, raised in Fort Lauderdale and Miami, Diego made his way to far West Texas in February of 2001. "I had a friend who worked in several different national parks. It sounded adventurous and interesting, so I gave it a shot. I had no idea where I was going until I got here. I got to Alpine on the train and thought that was it," he shares smiling. "I signed a four-month contract to work as a sous chef in Big Bend National Park and just never left. I fell in love with this beautiful area, but most of all, the community that dwells here.

"I met the love of my life, Sunnie Osborne, who worked the front desk in the park at the time when I worked there. We got married years later, and now both work at the Starlight. We've lived here year 'round for thirteen years. It never gets old or boring out here."

Diego started making chili when he first got to the basin [at Big Bend National Park] in 2001. "I was amazed at the way they make chili there: they just opened a can. Coming from Florida, chili wasn't a big deal there, and they put beans in, which I didn't think was that big of a deal." But even Diego knew that chili out of a can was criminal in Big Bend country. "I played around with dry ingredients to make a recipe. It was a step better than the stuff out of the can," Diego recalls. "And that was the start of it. Up there it's a different ball of wax. When you are cooking for the masses, you have to use a lot of prefab food. So, we changed it and made things more homemade.

"When I got to the Big Bend Motor Inn, I started learning from the Mexican ladies how to make chili. They called it 'chili bowl' because that's how it read on the menu. I would ask: 'what are you makin'?' and they would say: 'chili bowl.' They opened my eyes to using premade red chili sauce that was frozen instead of using chili powder or dry ingredients. So that was an improvement, but I still didn't think it was the best chili yet.

"Here at the Starlight, there were beautiful Mexican women making everything by hand. They taught me which fresh ingredients would be best for the chili. We started charring the tomatoes and jalapeños and onions. It gave the chili a roasted flavor. It had an excellent unique taste." Diego says they started making dried ancho chiles into a purée which was a step up from the canned stuff. He says, "I don't think there's anyone down here that does that, and you wouldn't be allowed to do that at the CASI cook-off." He says the CASI recipes are tightly regulated. Everyone must use the same dry ingredients and same cut of beef.

"After a while, Bill Ivey introduced me to his chili mix, so we incorporated it into the chili recipe on November 15, 2010. "I've never gone to the cook-off just for fun. It is fun, but we work. It's one of the busiest times of the year. The Starlight crew and I were vendors and sponsors. It means putting in twenty-hour days, but it is fun and worth it."

Although Diego hasn't had the opportunity to cook in the cook-off, he cooks for the masses that are there to enjoy the party. "When we sold our chili burgers, chili dogs, and Frito pies, we received countless compliments and comments about how our chili was better than anything they had judged yet. It's also one of our best-received items on our menu," he says. When cooking at the cook-off, the cooks normally camp onsite at Krazy Flats.

"What's weird is that they don't have chili for anyone to eat unless you're judging. If you're not judging, you ain't eating. Thousands of people show up, but yeah, there's no chili for them to buy. People are vending hot dogs and hamburgers. So we sold chili and boy, did we sell chili. Judges came by to ask how we made it. I explained how we char the vegetables. That's when I found out all the rules about it. It's not that easy to enter. You have to enter other cook-offs and be invited. There are about 150 people that compete—there were more in recent years (275 in 2014). We carried [chili in] five-gallon buckets over and ultimately sold twenty to thirty gallons.

"The best thing ever was developing a chili recipe for a chili wrestling competition," says Diego. He explains that they had to make sure it wasn't real chili as the wrestling competition actually took place in the concoction. "All I remember using was tofu," he says, "and making sure we didn't use any actual chili peppers—we didn't want any body parts to get burned! It was hilariously fun and silly."

Terlingua Ghostown Chili
Courtesy of Tom Dozier

"At Terlingua Ghostown Chili, we are committed to bringing delicious, authentic Texas Red to your home in a manner that is simple to prepare and absolutely tasty," says Tom. He won the CASI championship in 2010 and has several other notable wins under his belt. Check out his spices at www.ghostownchili.com.

Makes 4 to 6 servings

2 pounds of ground beef, or other ground meat
1 (8-ounce) can of tomato sauce
1 (14.5-ounce) can beef broth
1 cup of water
1 to 2 serrano peppers (optional)

Terlingua Ghostown Chili Seasoning (Spice Dump)
4 tablespoons of chili powder
1 tablespoon of light chili powder
2 teaspoons of onion powder
2 teaspoon of garlic powder
2 teaspoons of cumin
1/2 tablespoon of paprika
1/2 teaspoon of cayenne pepper
1/2 teaspoon of salt

Cook the ground meat in a large pot. Drain the meat and return to the pot.

Combine the tomato sauce, beef broth, and water. Bring the mixture to a boil.

Add the chili seasonings. For added heat poke holes in 1 to 2 serrano peppers and float them in the simmering chili for 30 minutes. Turn heat off. Remove the peppers or squeeze the juices into the chili careful not to add any seeds, as desired. Let the finished pot rest for 15 minutes and serve warm.

TOM DOZIER

Tom Dozier is the man behind Terlingua Ghostown Chili. He won the CASI competition in 2010 only two years after he started cooking on the chili trail, earning him plenty of credibility in the chili world. "I drive a street sweeper for the city of Irving," Tom shares. "I started cooking chili when my wife's cousin held a crock pot cook-off at her school. After that, I thought I knew how to cook, so I found a cook-off in town to see what it was all about and meet people at the same time." That was in 2008. Only one year later, Tom qualified through CASI to cook in Terlingua in 2009 for his first time. After winning the CASI championship in 2010, he placed second in 2011. "For some reason, I've been fortunate to win in this business. I don't know if it's luck or fate or what. My goal is to get Herman Everett or Deanna (Castillo) to win. I would love someone from the Terlingua area to win."

When he started Terlingua Ghostown Chili, he began by branding the name. "I made a one dump recipe with my spices," Tom says. "It's condensed from the recipe that Deanna and Herman make. If you go online, you can see it." During his research phase, Tom noticed he didn't recognize a lot of the names behind the major spice brands and felt encouraged that he too could be successful in the chili spice business. "There are so many people that sell chili out there that I have never heard of," Tom says. "So I say, 'I can do that.' And I have a good name—Terlingua Ghostown Chili—that people want to see. People know Terlingua for music and chili. My name (Tom Dozier) is on the other side (of the spice packet), but it's not even really on the label." Tom says he bases his whole business concept on the "really good" chili made in the Terlingua area. "You can't sell chili to a chili cook because they know how to cook it. So I sell mostly to people who want to [learn how to] cook," he laughs.

He says his friends Herman and Deanna keep him coming back to Terlingua. And the quietness of the area. "I also like that we don't have the Dallas traffic down there. I can relax out there and enjoy the chili," he says. There's a spirit of chili camaraderie that Tom exudes. "Sure I'd like to win another championship, but I'd love to see them win too [Herman and Deanna]," he says.

Terlingua Museum of Chili History Chili
Courtesy of Charlie Throop, Terlingua Museum of Chili History

"We had a lot of fun cooking chili," says Charlie. *"We passed out a Terlingua Museum of History card to all who would take one. It said: 'Yes, this is a collector's item.' Garbage men have been collecting them off the ground for years.*

Makes 6 to 8 servings

3 pounds lean ground chuck
1/2 cup water
1 (8-ounce) can Hunt's tomato sauce
2 tablespoons Hungarian paprika
1 tablespoon onion powder
1 tablespoon garlic powder
1/2 teaspoon cayenne
1 Knorr's beef cube
1 Knorr's chicken cube

Spice Dump
3 tablespoons Fort Worth light chili powder
3 tablespoons San Antonio chili powder
2 tablespoons Cowtown light chili powder
1 1/2 tablespoons cumin
1/2 teaspoon black pepper
1/2 teaspoon garlic powder
1/2 teaspoon salt
1 packet Sazón Goya seasoning mix

In a large pot, brown the ground meat in the water covering with the lid. Cook for 5 minutes and add the tomato sauce.

Cover the meat with the water. Add the paprika, onion powder, garlic powder, cayenne, beef cube, chicken cube. Add the Spice Dump. Cook for 20 minutes at a rolling boil. Serve.

CHARLIE THROOP

Born in Corsicana, Charlie now lives in Fulshear, Texas, and is retired from the Houston Fire Department. He talks about the first time he visited Terlingua. "I left out of a music festival workshop in Kerrville, Texas, and my neighbor John Billy Murray was supposed to be there cooking. I had a few days off, so I just drove out there." Charlie says that in 1984, the first year he drove out to Terlingua, John Billy just so happened to win first place.

Charlie has both cooked and competed in showmanship. "It's always a fun trip and fun folks," says Charlie. "I had known about it for a while, and there is so much other stuff to get into while you're there." He attended from '85 to '95 then took a nineteen-year break before coming back in 2014 with the same basic show he did before. "I never went out there and did not at least place in showmanship," says Charlie. "The trip itself is fun, and I like doing different things when I am out there."

He says his chili has indeed won a few awards but not enough to mention, "I mainly do these for the crowds and the fun of putting on a show," says Charlie. "The best cook-off was when I won first place in chili and first place in show at Onalaska, Texas, in 1986."

Texas 2-Alarm Chili
Courtesy of Tom Nall

Tom was an integral part of Wick Fowler's 2-Alarm Chili company for several years. Wick Fowler's Famous 2-Alarm Chili Kits contain a commercial version of the spice mix used in this recipe.

Makes 4 to 6 servings

2 pounds 85% lean beef, ground or diced (sugar cube-sized)
1/2 cup sweet Texas 1015 onion, diced
3 cloves garlic, diced
1/3 heaping cup fresh ground ancho chile pepper
1 (8-ounce) can tomato sauce, divided in half
4 ounces beef broth, plus 4 more ounces
4 ounces water, plus 4 more ounces
1 tablespoon oregano
1 tablespoon cumin
1 tablespoon salt
1 tablespoon paprika
Cayenne pepper*
1 fresh jalapeño, seeded, deveined, and diced
1 1/2 tablespoons of masa harina

Brown the beef in a large pot over medium-high heat. Do not drain the grease. Add the onion and garlic to the beef and sauté until the onion and garlic are opaque, approximately 5-10 minutes. Add the ground ancho chile pepper and simmer for 15 minutes more.

Add half the tomato sauce, first 4 ounces of the beef broth, and first 4 ounces of the water, and simmer for 15 minutes.

Mix the oregano, cumin, salt and paprika together. Stir into the chili and simmer for 15 minutes.

Add cayenne pepper and jalapeño. Mix the masa harina with the remaining water and stir until you have a smooth paste. Add the remaining beef broth, tomato sauce, and masa paste. Simmer for 30 minutes to an hour. If chili appears too thick for your liking, add more water or beer.

*Depending on the heat you desire, add 1 teaspoon of cayenne pepper for 1-Alarm Chili, add 2 teaspoons of cayenne for 2-Alarm Chili, or leave out the cayenne pepper all together for False Alarm Chili.

TOM NALL

In his book *Texas Cowboy Cookin': Tom Nall & Texas at the Smithsonian,* the story of "Texas Chuckwagon Chili" is recounted and reprinted here with the author's permission:

"Staples of the early Texas cattle drives were known to be bacon, ham hocks or salt pork, beans and coffee. Sometimes there might be a cold, hard biscuit on the menu, but most cowboys didn't count on such luxury. Though beef was on the hoof, it wasn't on the plate. But in the case of injury or even sickness to a steer, the "Cookie" might just butcher up that carcass and serve the boys beef-steak. Of course, the drives were moving. Idleness was costing ranchers and cowboys money, so the meat usually didn't have the time to be processed by smoking, salting or even drying for jerky. So it was served up fast before spoiling and going to complete waste.

"Now one method of some meat preparation was to marinate it in a broth of spices. This provided tenderization, some preservation, and most of all, flavor (these beeves could be somewhat "gamey!"). With the influence of the Mexican cowboy, the vaquero, chili spices might be added to the marinade. Many of the vaqueros traveled with their chiles. Or some chuckwagon cooks would plant herbs, spices, and chiles in thickets of mesquite trees so they might harvest their "crops" on return trips up these cattle trails. The mesquite trees with their thorny attachments acted as a barrier to some of the traveling cattle, horses and wagons as they journeyed north. The addition of chile spices to the tough diced beef of the cattle drives was how Texas Chili—the state dish—was invented."

Truett Airhart's Award-Winning Texas-Style Chili
Courtesy of Barbara Collins

This recipe uses a prepared chili mix seasoning package available from Airhart Enterprises at www.texaschilispice.com. "It's a simple, straightforward recipe that gives you room to explore adding different meats, vegetables, and flavors," says Barbara. "It's what you would imagine a cowboy would have in his saddlebag: easy to put together, a good filling meal. Pair my cornbread with this chili to calm the heat and give your palate both sweet and salty flavors."

Barbara recommends using the recipe below to make a Frito chili pie the original way—in a bag. And then add her cornbread. (For Barbara's Mexican Cornbread recipe, see page 164.)

Makes 4 to 6 servings

2 pounds beef
1 (8-ounce) can tomato sauce
2 (8-ounce) cans water
1 (3-ounce) package of Texas Style Chili Mix

Brown the beef in a frying pan and drain the grease. Place the meat into a 3-quart pot and add the tomato sauce and water. Cover and simmer until the meat is tender, approximately 10-15 minutes.

Add the chili mix and simmer an additional 30 minutes, stirring occasionally.

BARBARA COLLINS & TRUETT AIRHART

Stay at home mom, artist, blogger, and cook Barbara Collins has made her fair share of meals for the masses.

"We had a few weeks when the kids were in camp," Barbara shares, "so we went to Big Bend for the pleasure of seeing a new place." She had never been to the area but says her husband had traveled to Marfa once. "He had always wanted to stay in Alpine, Marfa, and Marathon, so we did. We stayed at the Gage and took day trips to the other cities. It was a really fun thing. We visited Lajitas and spent a few days there." She says they then visited Terlingua where they had dinner. "We just loved sitting on the porch and talking to people," Barbara says. Barbara and her husband William competed in a chili cook-off in Galveston while they were dating in the early '80s. After their marriage, the couple competed in that cook-off a few more times before the event outgrew its property. Although Barbara hasn't had the distinction of cooking at the Terlingua chili cook-off, she has had the honor of learning to make chili from Truett Airhart, a Terlingua chili cook-off aficionado.

"He [Truett] was friends with my dad, and he loved to cook. He was a lobbyist and would cook for senators. People in Washington, DC, would invite him to come barbecue for their events." Barbara says he met a lot of people and would cook for many of them for parties or events on the side. Although his first love was politics, he was almost busier cooking for his friends. "He traveled a lot between Houston and Washington," she says. "He settled in the Hill Country, and I still see him every once in a while. So the recipe I contributed is his recipe. It's easy, quick, good."

Barbara says he taught her how to make his chili, and he gave her a recipe for queso using his chili mix. She says the best part about her friendship with Truett is his stories—all the people he's met and his chili experience— how it started, how he won, what he won, etc. "I think the cutest thing about it is that he did it from his heart. He did it because he loved to cook and loved to make people happy with his food. To give you an example, I had a housewarming party, and he insisted on bringing a couple of briskets. Now he has this chili mix that he's trying to get into stores."

Truett lived at Barbara's dad's house when he was in Houston. "This was a tremendous help for us," Barbara shares, "because we knew he would make sure my dad was eating well. He would use Dad's house as a home base while he was traveling back and forth [to Washington, DC]. That's the kind of friend he is to our family."

Barbara says there's no secret to Truett's chili, but she says everything starts off better if you sauté some onions with it.

Truett Airhart's Award-Winning Texas-Style Chili, continued

"He doesn't call for onions, but I've added onions and have thrown in other things from time to time. I like adding fresh tomato in the summer, for example. You can use wild game with it, and it's awesome. That's what I like about this recipe: it's your base. It's like your roux in gumbo. It's a medium heat—not so spicy your mouth is on fire and you can't taste anything. Especially with a cold beer, it tastes great."

One thing Barbara loves about the recipe (as it claims on the package) is that it only takes about thirty minutes to make. One of Truett's tips was not to let the chili cook longer than the recommended thirty minutes. He said that it was even better to make the chili a day before, and reheat it the next day.

"It's such a simple recipe. It's fun to make. It's straightforward and easy, but it gives you an allowance if you want to explore with other meats, flavors, and vegetables. If you want it more garlicky, add more fresh garlic. It's not a lot of foo foo."

Venison Ribeye Chili
Courtesy of Rodney Simmons

*In the late '70s, Rodney was one of three teenage broth-
ers living with his parents in the town known at the time as
"Lajitas Trading Post." He submits this chili recipe which is
totally his own. The Simmons brothers' claim to fame is the
adoption and domestication of Clay Henry, the goat mayor
of Lajitas and a general store located on the banks of the Rio
Grande, some thirteen miles from the Terlingua ghost town.
The family left the trading post in the early '80s and moved
to Midland, Texas. "We liked the youngest goat the most, and
we named him after our friend from high school in Alpine,"
says Rodney. "His name was Clay; his dad was the principal at
the time. Clay Henry (the goat) grew up drinking soda pop.
One day, during a dance on the porch someone gave him a
beer and the rest is history! I developed the recipe over de-
cades, but basically, I ripped off a store bought chili mix and
improvised from there."*

*Rodney uses seared venison and grilled rib eye steak in his
recipe. He recommends cooking the meat over mesquite
wood with your choice of seasonings. He also recommends
roasting the tomatoes and hatch green chiles over the
mesquite wood as well. He recommends starting with four
tablespoons of red chili powder, so it's not too hot for kids.
He says to add more "if you're lookin' for your nose to run."
Rodney says it's best to let the chili rest overnight.*

*His view on the bean controversy? "A quote by Fowler,
Tolbert or Shelby, one of 'em said it," he says. "'Anybody that
knows beans about chili knows that chili ain't got no beans!'"*

Makes 4 to 6 servings

1 pound seasoned venison back strap*
1 pound seasoned thick-cut rib eye*
2 cups tomatoes*, smashed or processed
1/2 large red onion, diced
1 cup Hatch green chiles*, skinned, seeded, and chopped
6 cups beef broth
2 tablespoons comino
2 tablespoons roasted garlic, minced

Venison Ribeye Chili, continued

1 tablespoon sea salt
1 teaspoon fresh ground peppercorn medley
4 tablespoons fresh ground red chili powder**
1 small jalapeño, seeded and diced.

Garnish
Red onion, diced
Cheddar cheese, grated by hand

Cut the meat into 1/2- to 1-inch chunks and place into a large crockpot. Add all the remaining ingredients. Cover the crockpot with the lid, and set the temperature on high for 2 hours. After 2 hours, turn the temperature on the crockpot to low and allow to simmer for another 2 to 3 hours (or until the football game comes on).

Serve with fresh diced red onion and hand-grated cheese. This is very good and worth every bit of effort you put into it. Your guests will be amazed.

*Rodney recommends searing the backstrap, grilling the rib eye, and roasting the tomatoes and Hatch green chiles over mesquite wood.

**NOTE: these chiles can be extremely HOT. Make sure you get low to medium range regarding the level of heat. We want flavor not heat. The red chili powder brings the heat. Four tablespoons is a good starting place, and the kids can still eat it. Add more, if desired.

Wil's Green Chili
Courtesy of Wil Rothschild

*"Our restaurant is called Terlingua after the Texas town,"
shares Chef Wil of his Portland, Maine eatery. He says the
menu is a mish-mash of Tex-Mex, Caribbean, BBQ, and of
course, chili. "We do a couple of good chilies. The chili verde
is very popular and one of our best-selling dishes. It's done
New Mexico style, with our big barrel roasters for the
Anaheim chiles."*

Makes 6 to 8 servings

3 pounds Anaheim chiles
2 tablespoons vegetable oil
2 large Spanish onions, diced medium
4 cloves of garlic, minced
2 pounds boneless pork shoulder, cut into 3/4-inch cubes
1 cup of corn, freshly cut from cob
3 tablespoons kosher salt
1 gallon of water, 1 cup reserved
1 medium potato, diced medium
1 large tomato, diced medium
1/3 cup masa harina

Garnish
Barbecued pork shoulder or rib meat
Diced Vidalia onions
Cotija cheese
Scallions

Fire-roast the Anaheim peppers over an open flame. Cover
and let them sit for 20 minutes. Uncover and let them cool to
room temperature. Peel them and remove the stems and the
majority of the seeds. Chop the peppers finely.

In large, thick-bottomed pot add the oil and onions. Cook
over medium heat stirring constantly until onions just start to
caramelize. Add the garlic and cook for two more minutes.
Add the pork and cook, stirring occasionally until the juices
are nearly gone, and the ingredients start to sizzle. Add the
corn, salt, and water, reserving one cup of the water. Simmer
for 30 minutes.

Wil's Green Chili, continued

Add the Anaheim peppers and simmer for another 30 minutes or until the pork is fork-tender. Add the potato and simmer until the potato is very soft. Add the tomato.

Whisk the remaining cup of water with masa and stir into chili. Return the chili to a simmer to thicken. Garnish with above toppings and serve with grilled flatbread brushed with melted butter and honey.

WIL ROTHSCHILD

Enamored with the Texas town, owners Pliny and Melanie Reynolds were inspired to name their first restaurant Terlingua. Ironically Chef Wil has traveled throughout the Southwest but hasn't made it to Terlingua, Texas.

"I've come close," Wil says. "I've been cooking for twenty years all over the country: California, Colorado, Vermont, Maine, the Bahamas. I hooked up with Pliny and Melanie through friends we had in common." He says that Pliny was opening a restaurant and he [Wil] was looking for a good place to work. "We've been jam-packed ever since we opened [in the summer of 2015]."

"Out in Colorado, there are a lot of green chilies. I traveled in New Mexico and developed a taste for this pork green chili. So the recipe I shared is an adaptation of my favorite styles with my own flair. My sister-in-law is a farmer and makes really good cheese, so I top it with that and some of our BBQ pork shoulder. It has sweet corn and potato and a little kick to it, but it's a nice dish."

The Terlingua restaurant is a boutique BBQ restaurant that combines house-smoked meats with Latin American fare. In addition to Wil's Green Chili, you might want to try their smoked brisket sweet potato hash, deviled egg sandwich, chilaquiles, ghost pepper pork belly wraps, poblano cheddar grits or their roasted butternut squash empanada.

You Can't Beat it Chili*
Courtesy of Blue Jay Murphy

Blue Jay says browning the chili meat in chorizo grease gives the chili a distinct flavor. He says the key to keeping the meat from sticking is to remove it to a stainless steel pot once it's browned. He built his own special pot from a nitrogen cylinder that's round on the bottom.

Blue Jay says to check the chili often to make sure it doesn't dry out. If it does, he recommends adding beer to the chili. When he is cooking competition chili, he likes to use whichever beer is sponsoring the cook-off, but when he is at home he uses whatever beer is in his hand. He prefers to use a dark German beer because it gives the chili a stouter flavor.

Blue Jay says not to make the chili too hot. He uses mole to cut any sweetness and cool the heat. He cooks the chili until it's quite thick, so thick that a spoon will stand up in it.

*Read the Cook's Notes at the end of the recipe before making this chili.

Makes 12 to 14 servings

1/4 pound chorizo, grease reserved
5 pounds of lean chuck, cut into 1/4-inch cubes
2 pounds of thick cut pork chops or pork shoulder, cut into 1/4-inch cubes
2 large red or white onions, diced
8 to 10 large cloves garlic, minced
1 (8-ounce) can tomato sauce
2 (14.5-ounce) cans beef broth
2 cans dark German beer
7 tablespoons chili powder
4 tablespoons cumin
2 tablespoons paprika
2 tablespoons MSG
2 tablespoons ground chile seeds
1 tablespoon oregano
1 tablespoon sugar
1 tablespoon mole

Brown the chorizo over medium heat in a large pan. Remove cooked chorizo from the pan with a slotted spoon and

You Can't Beat it Chili, continued

reserve for another use. Do not discard the chorizo grease. Brown the beef and pork in the same pan with the chorizo grease.

Once the meats are browned, remove them to a stainless steel pot to prevent the meat from sticking.

Add all the remaining ingredients to the pot except for the mole, and bring the chili to a boil. Once boiling, decrease the heat to a simmer, stirring occasionally. Cook about 5 hours. It will cook faster if you stir it more frequently. Make sure it doesn't dry out. Add beer or water, as needed.

Before all the moisture is gone, add the mole. Serve with tortilla chips.

Cook's Notes:

Meat: You can ask the butcher to grind your meat into a chili grind (thicker than ground meat). At home, you can use the meat in chunks, but in competition you need the consistency to be the same.

Tomato paste: You can use fresh tomatoes, but they take more work and for home chili it's fine, but for competition chili you can't use them because fresh tomato seeds won't cook down and they will take points off.

Dark German beer: I use whatever beer is sponsoring the chili cook-off, but if it's for me at home, I prefer a dark, German beer because it makes for a stouter flavor.

Chili powder: I grind my own, but you can buy good chili powder if you go to Hatch, New Mexico on Labor Day. I always buy chili powder there and 4-5 bushels [of peppers] that they roast there. I take a big ice chest and take them home for the winter and do stuffed chiles.

Cumin: I grind the comino seeds. It's fresher than buying ground cumin, but either one will work.

Mole: You can buy mole in any Mexican grocery store, but I use unsweet dark chocolate found in the chocolate aisle or herbs/spice aisle. Blue Jay says that the mole gives the chili a nice, dark, rich color.

BLUE JAY MURPHY

"Beans are a side dish," says Blue Jay. "There is a reason for that: the old cowboys said if you mixed your beans with your chili, the beans will just become mush and mess up the chili. At cook-offs, having beans in your chili disqualifies you. Blue Jay says even a stray jalapeño seed can cause a competitor to lose points during judging. He says the only thing the judges should be able to see is "the seasoned meat and the sauce."

Blue Jay suggests making three to four gallons at a time because you can freeze it in the wintertime. "In the old days," he says "everybody cooked two to three gallons, and everybody got a taste, not just the judges." He competed with the First Church of Harley Davidson Rolling Motorcycles and Flying Chili Team. "We rode motorcycles and flew airplanes and had a good time," Blue Jay shares. "My friend and I both became ministers for twenty dollars in the FreeLife Church out in California. We actually performed weddings," he laughs.

In the early '70s and '80s, Blue Jay and his chili team would walk around the bars on Friday and Saturday nights before the bars closed at midnight asking folks, "Do you want to go to church services tonight?" "If they did," he says, "we would take two dollars from them and give them a cup with our initials on it." Then he says at around eleven o'clock, they would use the collected money to go out and buy more beer. That way the party didn't have to end at midnight. He says they would reconvene somewhere and drink until 2 a.m.

Terlingua was formerly a mining town and old mineshafts are peppered throughout the ghost town. While it is not considered safe to walk through them, they are open and easy to find. Periodically people will go exploring in the mineshaft caves and some have gone missing over the years. One year, Blue Jay says he and his friends camped down at the mineshafts. Blue Jay recalls the quartz hanging from the ceiling and the "cactus tea" (known for it's psychedelic properties) making the rounds among the group. "When we came out," he says, "we learned we had been in the cave for four days and had completely missed the cook-off."

CHILI ACCOMPANIMENT RECIPES

Chili is a strong dish that tends to stand alone, but if you need sides, salads, sauces or something sweet to go alongside, the chili cooks have shared some of their favorite accompaniment recipes.

Barbara's Mexican Cornbread
Courtesy of Barbara Collins

"This recipe was given to me by my housekeeper that helped me when I was raising my children," says Barbara. "She taught me three or four recipes, and this one has been a winner in my family every time. My family will boycott Thanksgiving if I don't make it. When we lived in Colorado, I made it often. I brought it to one party where a man tasted it, loved it, and asked every single person at the party who made the cornbread. When he found out it was me, he said he needed the recipe because it was just like his grandmother's in Mexico. And because it's so easy to memorize and share, I gave it to him on the spot.."

Makes about 15-20 servings

2 cups Pioneer brand cornmeal
2 eggs
1 cup corn oil or vegetable oil
2 (14.75-ounce) cans cream style corn
1 (14-ounce) can sweetened condensed milk

Preheat oven to 400 degrees F.

Mix everything together in a 13 by 9-inch pan. Bake 30 to 40 minutes until golden brown.

Let the cornbread cool for about 20 to 30 minutes and then cut it into little squares.

Cook's Notes: "What's interesting about this cornbread is that it is almost better the second day. It's great for breakfast. It's great cold. I've discovered it rises pretty thick, so you can take it and cut it in half through the middle like a bagel, then put it in an iron skillet and griddle it with a little butter for three minutes, turn it off, and let it sit on the stove," says Barbara.

Barbara also makes this suggestion. "After you've eaten your meal, put a scoop of Blue Bell vanilla ice cream on top of the griddled cornbread. I would never think my cornbread and ice cream would go together, but it's insanely incredible."

And she recommends these ideas. "The cornbread slices can be smashed into patties and griddled for breakfast too. My nephew wants me to figure out how to wrap it around a hot dog and deep fry it to make a corn dog."

Cadillac Cowgirl Enchilada Gravy
Courtesy of Kelly Brignon

"This recipe is part of our Christmas Eve tradition," shares Kelly. "We serve it with tamales and rice, but you can serve it over enchiladas, burritos, or even eggs as a breakfast dish! We've been enjoying this meal for several years, and it's a great way to warm up during the winter months. It's the perfect comfort food."

Makes 4 to 6 servings (enough to cover 12 enchiladas)

1/2 pound ground chuck
4 cloves garlic, minced
1 large yellow onion, minced
1/2 cup water, plus 2 cups
1/2 cup vegetable oil
1/2 cup all purpose flour
2 cups beef broth
2 1/2 cups water, divided
2 tablespoons San Antonio red chili powder
1 tablespoon Stockyards Special chili powder
1/8 teaspoon Terlingua Dust hot chile pepper powder
1 1/2 teaspoons cumin
2 teaspoons salt
1 teaspoon Tellicherry pepper (black pepper)

In a saucepan or stockpot, combine the ground chuck, minced garlic and onion and a 1/2 cup water. Bring the mixture to a boil, cover, and decrease the heat to a simmer. Cook for 30 minutes or until meat is tender.

In a separate hot skillet, add the vegetable oil. When the oil is heated through, add the flour, lower the heat, and whisk the oil and flour together until the mixture is smooth and golden in color.

Add this mixture to the beef along with the beef broth, the remaining two cups of water, and all of the spices. Stir together until combined, and cook over medium-low heat until the mixture has thickened into a gravy-like consistency. Taste and adjust seasonings as necessary.

El Diablo Cornbread with Sausage
Courtesy of Tom Dozier

This cornbread has a Cajun twist you'll love.

Makes about 12 to 15 servings

1 cup yellow cornmeal
1 teaspoon salt
1 teaspoon baking soda
1 cup milk
2 eggs
1/2 cup vegetable oil
1 can cream style corn
1 (10-ounce) block mild cheddar cheese, grated
1/2 cup jalapeños, chopped
1 large onion, chopped
1 medium red bell pepper, chopped
1 cup andouille sausage, sautéed
1 teaspoon Slap Ya Mama Seasoning

Preheat oven to 350 degrees F.

In a large bowl, mix the cornmeal, salt, and baking soda. Add the milk, eggs, vegetable oil, and cream style corn and stir. Add the remaining ingredients. Stir to combine.

Grease the bottom of a 9 by 11-inch pan, and pour the mixture into the pan. Bake the cornbread for 55 minutes. Let cool for at least 30 minutes before serving.

Garlic Cheesy Beer Bread
Courtesy of Wally Roberts

This recipe won first place at the Terlingua Dutch Oven Cook-Off. Wally says the key to the bread is using the cheapest beer possible.

Makes 24 servings

4 cups all purpose flour
2 tablespoons baking powder
2 tablespoons garlic salt
2 cubes chicken bouillon
1 tablespoon sugar
1 cup grated cheese
2 beers

Mix all the dry ingredients together, then mix in the cheese. Add just enough beer to make a stiff dough. Knead five times and let the dough rise for one hour in a warm spot.

Preheat the oven to 400 degrees. Pinch off 1 1/2-inch by 1 1/2-inch pieces, careful not to pack the dough. Place the dough onto a baking sheet or into a Dutch oven with a one-inch space between each roll. Cook 10 to 15 minutes until golden brown.

Cook's Note: If it is too cool for the dough to rise soak a towel with hot water, squeeze the water out and cover the dough. Repeat every 15 minutes until the dough rises.

WALLY ROBERTS

Wally Roberts of "Wally's Pole and Grill" in Krazy Flats, a special area at the CASI site, has enjoyed several years of cowboy camp cooking. He shared a story he wrote about his daughter Sarah and her first time competing in Dutch oven cooking at Terlingua. It is reprinted here with his permission.

Sarah's First Cook-off
Written by Wally Roberts

My daughter Sarah has been helping me camp cook since she was too small to pick up a Dutch oven. When Sarah was twelve years old, we spotted a flier for the Terlingua International Dutch oven cook-off. Terlingua is best known for a chili cook-off, but this Dutch oven cook-off was advertised as a family event.

Sarah and I had never competed in any kind of cooking competition and didn't know what to expect. We were not sure what to take and didn't want to lug our cook rig all the way down to this ghost town—a stone's throw from the Mexican border. We just loaded my fire pit, some supplies, and a couple of ovens. Once we got there, we set up a table to work on along with the tailgate of my old truck. We also put our custom made aprons on that Robbie handmade just for this event and went to cooking.

This competition was very well managed and had a double-blind judging system for the thirty-five teams entered. I tended the fires and Sarah decided what she was going to cook for each category. She had to come up with an authentic Dutch oven main course, dessert, and bread. Sarah at twelve was a skinny little girl with long blond hair and an eternal smile on her face. Sarah went to work, mixing, and concocting the courses. Everyone was amazed this little girl was out there putting ingredients together like chicken, pecans, and making sauces with butter and herbs then grabbing the cast iron Dutch ovens to cook in. Dad just made sure the coals would be ready when needed. All the other contestants and spectators came by, called Sarah by name, and asked her where she was from and how long she had been cooking. Sarah would tell them all about our trail-riding adventures and catering jobs.

Sarah cooked a pot roast for the main, a cobbler with a beautifully weaved top for the dessert, and invented a beer bread recipe for the bread entry. Sarah closely watched the time, so the entries came off just right to be perfectly cooked and make the turn in time.

Preparation, timing, and heat distribution were right on track; our turn-ins looked delicious and were cooked to perfection.

As we anxiously waited for the results to be tallied, we sat and listened to Mike Blakely play guitar and sing cowboy songs.

Finally, the results were in. All the teams gathered close to hear the announcer. Third, second, and first for the main and dessert went by with no luck. Third and second for bread was announced. I looked at Sarah to get ready to console hurt feelings, then BINGO, Sarah's number was called for first place with "Sarah Roberts's Garlic Cheesy Beer Bread." Sarah jumped up to go collect her first place award and check. This competition was an open competition with no youth division. Sarah was competing against teams of cooks who had cooked for more than fifty years in Dutch ovens.

One of the funniest things that happened during this event was when Sarah and I were sitting with all the other cooks waiting for results to be read. Sarah looked at me and quietly said, "Dad, how do all these people know my name? Everyone that comes up to me already knows me, and I don't know them." I smiled at my little girl and pointed to her apron, which had in big letters on her chest "SARAH." Robbie wanted to make sure we looked good as a team, and custom made Sarah's apron with her name on it just like mine.

After the cook-off we put up all our supplies, burned and oiled our Dutch ovens, and went back to the hotel room to get ready for the evening. We wanted to have some fun, and the only place to go out in Terlingua is the La Kiva. La Kiva is an underground bar and grill where motorcycle rallies and outlaws come to hang out. We sat at the bar with some other families there to visit Big Bend swapping stories and getting to know people. There were a couple of 17 and 18-year old sisters with their dad, and the two girls got into an arm wrestling contest. Sarah (at 12 years old) didn't have a problem challenging the winner to a match. The two girls squared off, put their elbows on the bar, and locked hands. The older girl was twice Sarah's size but did not have half the determination. The older girl's dad said go: Sarah struggled a little but quickly put the big girl down, looked around the bar and said, "Who's next?"

Kathleen's Salsa
Courtesy of Kathleen Tolbert Ryan

"I started making salsa at the first Tolbert's in the 1970s," Kathleen remembers. *"This salsa recipe is similar but not exactly the same ingredients. The serrano adds an extra kick. Then in the 1980s, I made a lot of salsa at home while pregnant with my second son Steven. It made him have some extra kicks during that time. Now he adores salsa."*

Yields 3 cups

2 (28-ounce) cans of whole peeled tomatoes
4 cloves garlic
2 jalapeños
1 serrano pepper
1/2 cup of cilantro
1/3 cup fresh lime juice
1/2 teaspoon light chili powder
1/2 teaspoon ground cumin
1/2 teaspoon sea salt

Drain the whole peeled tomatoes in a colander. Add some of the tomatoes, the garlic, and the peppers to a blender, and blend on chop. Then add the cilantro and lime juice, and blend in the remaining tomatoes. Pour into a large bowl and mix in the spices.

Miss Jenny's Cornbread
Courtesy of Jenny Turner

"I've spent my whole life eating dry cornbread, slathering it with butter and honey to help it go down, all the while searching for a moist, flavorful pairing to my ranch beans or brisket chili at Come & Take It BBQ," Jenny shares. "This is it."

Makes 12 servings

1 cup shredded cheddar cheese
3/4 cup buttermilk
1/4 cup melted butter
2 eggs, slightly beaten
1 can (8.5-ounce) cream-style corn
1 can (4.5-ounce) chopped green chiles, or jalapénos, diced
1 cup cornmeal
1 cup all purpose flour
2 teaspoons baking powder
1/2 teaspoon salt

Heat the oven to 375 degrees F. Generously spray a 9 by 11-inch baking pan with cooking spray (I prefer Baker's Joy).

Mix the cheese, buttermilk, melted butter, eggs, corn, and green chiles in a large bowl. In a separate bowl, mix the cornmeal, flour, baking powder, and salt. Add to the cheese mixture and stir until moist. Pour the batter into the prepared baking pan.

Bake for 40 to 50 minutes until the cornbread is lightly browned on top, and a toothpick inserted in the center comes out clean. Cool 10 minutes. Remove from pan and serve warm.

Orange Dreamsicle Jello Salad
Courtesy of Edward Hambleton

Ed from the Texas Chili Queens food truck in Austin, Texas, shares this nostalgic dessert.

Makes about 4 cups

1 3/4 cups water
2 boxes orange Jello (to make four cups total)
1 (12-ounce) can evaporated milk
2 cups canned mandarin oranges, drained

Boil the water and stir into the Jello until the Jello is dissolved. Quickly whisk in the evaporated milk. Refrigerate the mixture for 1 hour or until slightly thickened.

Remove the Jello mixture from the refrigerator. Stir in the mandarin oranges and pour into a mold or individual serving dishes. Refrigerate for at least 2 more hours before serving.

EDWARD HAMBLETON

Ed was born in Austin, Texas. "During childhood my family moved to Dallas, so I mostly grew up in Dallas," he says. "I went away to college in New York City and worked there for five years before coming back to Austin."

Ed owns and operates the Texas Chili Queens, a food truck in Austin that has guys selling chili in drag attire. "I was working in Austin and rediscovering the cuisine," he shares. "Part of that Texana food is Frito pie. So I organized a Frito pie Thanksgiving, and I made the chili. Everyone else brought other things. I was researching recipes and became intrigued by the chili queens' history. At the time, there was no other chili food truck, and it is ideal food-truck food. With the queens theme, I thought: we need a twenty-first-century twist, a new kind of queen—a drag queen. So the Texas Chili Queens food truck concept was born.

"When you hear about them [the original San Antonio chili queens], if you describe a chili queen it sounds like a drag queen—they are fun, flirtatious women, they work late at night, they are a tourist attraction more or less—they were exotic, spicy women who created exotic, spicy food. They were bawdy but also business women on the front lines making a life for themselves—so why not bring the original Texas food back to the streets of the capital with a twenty-first-century twist?

"I have not been to the cook-off," Ed shares. "I am interested in it. It's funny because with the original chili queens—women were making it, it was women's food—but when popular culture started producing large scale cook-offs, we had these big masculine guys and a hyper-masculine representation of chili, and I'm trying to bring back the feminine touch to the dish. Cook-off culture is interesting in that gender dynamic."

"Growing up, I always had a culinary interest," Ed says. "College is where I really blossomed as a cook and chef. I was the personal assistant to a chef in New York City: Shirley King. She was the nation's foremost fish expert, wrote the Williams-Sonoma fish cookbook, and more. As her personal assistant, we hit it off and became great friends. I moved in with her for the summer." He says Shirley brought him into the kitchen, and he started cooking more. They threw dinner parties together, and Ed's confidence in his cooking abilities grew as a result.

At the food trailer, Ed says their classic San Antonio chili is thick. "We harken back to chili queen chili: meat, simmered with chiles. So it's very thick. We have other varieties with beans and tomatoes that are soupy and stewy." Their best seller is the Classic San Antonio. Ed says the main ingredients are beef, pork, chili purée, and seasonings.

Skillet Cornbread
Courtesy of Mirt Foster

Sweet whole corn gives this cornbread texture.

Makes about 10-12 servings

2 packages Jiffy Brand cornbread mix
2 eggs
1 cup milk
1 (8.5-ounce) can whole kernel corn, drained
1 (4.5-ounce) can green chiles, diced
1/2 cup grated cheddar cheese
1 tablespoon canola oil
2 tablespoons butter

Heat the oven to 350 degrees F. I like to use a cast-iron skillet, but an 8 by 10-inch pan will do just fine.

In a bowl, combine the cornbread mix, eggs, and milk. Fold in the corn, chiles, and cheese and set aside.

On the stovetop, warm the oil in a skillet or a pan on medium heat for 1 to 2 minutes. Turn off the heat, and pour the cornbread mixture into the hot pan. This technique gives the cornbread a crunchy bottom. Bake for 20 to 30 minutes or until golden brown. Remove the cornbread from the oven and dot lightly with butter.

Texas Southern Fried Pies
Courtesy of Tom Nall

In his book "Texas Cowboy Cookin': Tom Nall & Texas at the Smithsonian," Tom talks about fried pies: "Fried pie history is sketchy, but they are a southern tradition and came about as a way for frugal cooks to use every bit of food. Before cold storage and imports made fruits available year round, folks sliced up apples, peaches, apricots, etc. and then dried them, which is an effective means for long-term preservation. Many of those dried fruits ended up as fried pies."

For convenience, you can use store bought pie crusts that usually come two to the box and are found in the dairy section at the grocers.

Makes 6 to 8 servings

1 package of dried apricots, apples or peaches, as desired
1/2 cup water
1 cup powdered sugar, plus additional powdered sugar for dusting
1 tablespoon sugar
1 tablespoon vanilla
1 can high quality fruit pie filling, same fruit as the dried fruit chosen above
2 store bought piecrusts
butter
2 cups vegetable oil

In a saucepan add the dried fruit, water, powdered sugar, sugar, and vanilla. Bring to a boil.

Lower the heat and cook until the fruit is soft and the sugar water is reduced to a thick syrup. Drain the fruit pie filling and dice the fruit. Stir in 1/2 of the diced fruit into the saucepan with the dried fruit mixture.

Spread out one piecrust on a floured surface and cut it into four equal parts. Form each part into a round circle of flat dough. In each circle, place the pats of butter in the center of the dough, and then spoon in 2 tablespoons of the fruit mix

Texas Southern Fried Pies, continued

ture. Fold the dough over to form a crescent or half circle, cutting away the excess dough as needed. Slightly moisten the edges with water and press the edges to seal. Dip a fork into flour. With the floured tines of the fork, crimp the edges of each pie.

Set a cooking rack on a large baking sheet. Heat 2 to 3 inches of oil in a 4- to 5-quart cast-iron pot over medium heat until the oil begins to spit a little. (It will crackle if you put a pinch of flour in it.) Fry the pies, turning occasionally, until a deep golden brown. Transfer to a rack to cool and drain. Repeat this process with the second piecrust.

Dust the pies with the extra powdered sugar before serving.